MORAL DILEMMAS IN THE MAHĀBHĀRATA

MORAL DILEMMAS IN THE MAHĀBHĀRATA

Edited by

BIMAL KRISHNA MATILAL

INDIAN INSTITUTE OF ADVANCED STUDY
RASHTRAPATI NIWAS, SHIMLA
in association with
MOTILAL BANARSIDASS PUBLISHERS
PRIVATE LIMITED • DELHI (INDIA)

2nd Reprint : Delhi, 2014
First Published 1989

ISBN: 978-81-208-0603-0

MOTILAL BANARSIDASS
41 U.A. Bungalow Road, Jawahar Nagar, Delhi 110 007
8 Mahalaxmi Chamber, 22 Bhulabhai Desai Road, Mumbai 400 026
203 Royapettah High Road, Mylapore, Chennai 600 004
236, 9th Main III Block, Jayanagar, Bangaluru 560 011
Sanas Plaza, 1302 Baji Rao Road, Pune 411 002
8 Camac Street, Kolkata 700 017
Ashok Rajpath, Patna 800 004
Chowk, Varanasi 221 001

Published by the Secretary
INDIAN INSTITUTE OF ADVANCED STUDY
Rashtrapati Niwas, Shimla 171005

in association with
MOTILAL BANARSIDASS PUBLISHERS (P) LTD,
41 U.A. Bungalow Road, Jawahar Nagar, Delhi-110007

Printed in India
by RP Jain at NAB Printing Unit,
A-44, Naraina Industrial Area, Phase I, New Delhi–110028

CONTENTS

PREFACE

THERE is something rather special about the role of epic literature in Indian life. Is it the antiquity of the text that holds people in thrall or is it not rather the characters, many of whom are undoubtedly of archetypal stature? The situations in which an Agamemnon, a Jephtha or a Brutus found themselves do not seem to have gripped the imagination in the way in which the fate of a Sitā, a Draupadī or a Yudhiṣṭhira haunts us. Are such epic heroes and heroines role models for everyday life? Is there something universal about the dilemmas in which they found themselves? These questions are worth discussing.

We also need to explore the whole question of the relation between the mythopoeic and the moral in the context of the *Mahābhārata*. Here we have a story of extreme complexity, characters that are unforgettable, and a cosmic context in which gods and men alike grapple with destiny. The obligations of kinship and friendship jostle with each other. The women characters, as in everyday life, seem to bear a very heavy load of the burden of life and to stand in a key position in almost every conflict. We are presented with predicaments at every turn. At times these predicaments seem to be *aggravated* by social structure. At other times they are *cushioned* by it. At all events it may be proper to ask to what extent modern man living in the midst of a different set of social institutions can respond to all this. If he *can* so respond, it looks as if moral issues can be discussed apart from the context in which they arise. This would be a rather startling inference to make. There is an aside. What exactly have audiences in Avignon, Glasgow and elsewhere responded to as they watched Peter Brook's dramatic presentation of the *Mahābhārata*? An experimental piece of stagecraft, another piece of exotica, or what? Philosophical tangles tied up with *karma* and *dharma* are interwoven with the mythopoeic material. Perhaps philosophical issues are pinpointed rather more than they are in Greek epic literature. This could be debated by those concerned with comparative literature and comparative philosophy. How do the events described in the *Mahābhārata* compare with accounts of, say, the Trojan Wars, or with the story of the tribulations of Job? How much does historicity matter when we compare narratives?

In the *Mahābhārata*, we find a portrayal of bondage and also a transfiguration of bondage. The realism of it all lies in its recognition that suffering continues. There is no end to it. The heroes fear neither life nor death. Their ethos is a tough-minded one. We see men, women, kings, beggars, even gods, experiencing sorrow, hardship and disaster. Even in battle the winner has a hollow victory. The society portrayed in the epic much resembles what we find in the *Iliad*, with the gods of Greece rather more prone to interfere than those of the Indian pantheon. In her book on the *Mahābhārata*, Iravati Karve, the anthropologist, writes and I quote:

> All human efforts are fruitless, all human life ends in frustration; was the *Mahābhārata* written to drive home this lesson? Human toil, expectations, hates, hardships—all seem puny and without substance, like withered leaves eddying in the summer wind.

But isn't it the case that neither philosophers, nor dramatists kept up this view? Bharata, the first dramatic theorist, laid down the rule that a play must not end tragically; and extraordinarily enough, if we think of what some philosophers think it their business to do today (verbal traps having been substituted for cosmic ones), a large proportion of classical Indian philosophers assumed it was their job to show man the *way out* of bondage. If it were not for the *Gītā*, would the message of the *Mahābhārata* be closer to that of the Stoics than to that of classical Indian philosophers? In any case, we are led back to the theme of moral dilemmas time and again. The papers in this volume deal with this theme from the perspectives of both Indian philosophy and literature, inviting the reader to ponder afresh on a very important part of our common heritage.

MARGARET CHATTERJEE

INTRODUCTION

THESE papers were presented at a rather unusual colloquium at the Indian Institute of Advanced Study, Shimla, on Moral Dilemmas in the *Mahābhārata*. All credit undoubtedly goes to the present director, Professor Margaret Chatterjee, who has made this possible. In 1970, when I was teaching at the University of Pennsylvania, I was awarded a fellowship of this Institute by the then director, Dr Niharranjan Ray. But, unfortunately, due to circumstances beyond my control, I was unable to come. Better late than never. I thank the present director for inviting me as a Fellow, a dream fulfilled after eighteen years.

The topic is rather an outstanding one, not a bit less daring and intriguing. It takes courage and imagination to look at this great epic with a very different, presumably novel, perspective. But Professor Chatterjee has taken the necessary steps. While the previous directors of the Institute might have had dilemmas, moral or non-moral, in conducting the affairs of the IIAS, Professor Chatterjee has cut the Gordian knot, and resolved the second-order dilemma in choosing the subject, Moral Dilemmas in the *Mahābhārata*.

* * *

Peter Della Santina's paper gives a very illuminating appraisal of the concept of *dharma* as it was understood in the Śramaṇa and the Buddhist tradition. He contrasts the Brāhmanical view of *dharma* with that of the Buddhists. He gives a brilliant analysis of the first two chapters of the *Bhagavadgītā*, and interprets the conflict therein in terms of a controversy between Buddhism and Brāhmaṇism. I believe he is right, although Buddhism was not explicitly mentioned in the text.

Moral dilemmas may provoke two or three types of reaction

from the moral agent. Either he can give up action completely and choose the path of renunciation,* preferred by the Śramaṇa tradition, or he can choose to act without regard for the consequences. Kṛṣṇa's advice was not to give up actions but to rid oneself of one's desires for the fruits of any actions (*niṣkāmakarma*).

T.S. Rukmani's paper talks about the difficulties in identifying the cases of moral dilemmas in the *Mahābhārata*. She talks about the conflict of duties faced by various major characters: Yudhiṣṭhira, Bhīṣma, Kuntī, Vidura, and Gāndhārī. It is interesting to note that she quotes from the Gadāparvan the list of misdeeds perpetrated by Kṛṣṇa, which were enumerated by Duryodhana on his deathbed. Even a man like Duryodhana should not have died in the way he did. The poet Vyāsa makes up for it by relating in the last chapter how Duryodhana ascended to heaven, even before the Pāṇḍavas.

Dubey describes the epic as a representation of a major clash found in human society from time immemorial. It is the conflict between moral integrity and the need for survival as well as economic prosperity. The Kauravas did not care for what is ordinarily known as moral integrity, but they had their own pride. Besides, they wanted to protect their throne at any cost. One feels that there was some sort of integrity even in Duryodhana, although he was blinded by greed for possession and hatred against the Pāṇḍavas. The Pāṇḍavas were supposed to represent the virtue of moral integrity, but, as the story unfolded, they violated the code of moral integrity more often than not. They had, of course, suffered from regret and remorse. Dubey identifies three characters who did not experience moral dilemmas and consequently no regrets or remorse—Duryodhana, Karṇa, and Kṛṣṇa. He is right. But I believe that Kṛṣṇa perhaps did have some regret for the choices he made on behalf of the Pāṇḍavas. Unlike the other two, he fully understood the unresolvability of some moral dilemmas.

Referring to the gambling episode which is the centrepiece of the *Mahābhārata* story, S.M. Kulkarni calls Draupadī's problem an unresolved dilemma. I believe the dilemma of Draupadī is not only unresolved but also unresolvable as most moral dilemmas

* Cf. *Karma, Bhagavadgītā*, chap. ii.

are. However, there are certain legal implications which Kulkarni has briefly pinpointed in his short paper.

Can wives be regarded as chattels? Can they be gambled away? Can the husband, having lost his own freedom first, gamble with his wife's freedom? All these questions arise from the text itself. A discussion of all these issues will take a very long time which is not available in the context.

The second point is also interesting. If Śakuni cheated Yudhiṣṭhira in the game of dice and Yudhiṣṭhira did not claim that he had been cheated, even when this was openly known to him, would Śakuni be morally reprehensible? I believe he could be, but he would not be legally condemned. A fraudulent transaction would be invalid, although some would say that we should blame Yudhiṣṭhira equally for his actions.

Jani's paper deals with the social acceptability of the practice of polyandry as exemplified by the marriage of Draupadī. It seems that the moral repugnance against this practice was as evident in the days of the epic as it is today. Yudhiṣṭhira found it hard to convince Drupada and his son about the propriety of such a practice. Vyāsa's services were requisitioned to support the proposal. Yudhiṣṭhira referred to the practice of the ancient forefathers. However, the society that represented the metropolitan culture of the land of the Kurus and Pāñcālas found polyandry obnoxious, although polygamy was accepted as a norm in the royal families. As Drupada said: 'A prince must have many wives, but a princess must not have many husbands.' At some point, Yudhiṣṭhira countered Drupada by saying that polyandry must be a *dharma*, because he himself thought it was right, and he never thought an *adharma* to be right.

Polyandry was in some form or other prevalent in many societies in ancient times all over the world. It is still present among the Toḍas of the Nīlgiri Mountains, the Nairs of Kerala, and among some tribes in the Himalayan region. There may be many sociological explanations, which Jani talks about. He thinks that the Pāṇḍavas might have originally come from the Himalayan region, and so there was a conflict between the moral codes of the Pāṇḍavas and the Kauravas from the beginning. The suggestion that the Pāṇḍava family came from the Himalayan region is interesting, but the evidence to support it seems to be insufficient.

E.R. Sreekrishna Sarma approaches the epic from a slightly different point of view. He quotes from the *Dhvanyāloka* of the great poetician, Ānandavardhana, and says that the dominant *rasa* (mood or sentiment) in the *Mahābhārata* is *śānta* (quietitude). This mood usually leads to the saintly indifference towards all worldly pleasure or pain, and thereby leads to the path of *mokṣa*. The story is supposed to be a grand account of heroism and victory. But, ironically, it is the story of a great tragedy, where nobody becomes happy, and nobody achieves any glory—neither the victorious nor the vanquished. Sreekrishna Sarma says that the author has a subtle ironical smile as he goes on to describe the despondence, frustration, and confusion of such great heroes as Arjuna and Yudhiṣṭhira.

Kantawala's paper on *niyoga* discusses a very interesting social issue which has moral implications. Paternity was a great problem in the ancient royal family. Vyāsa was appointed to copulate with the two widow queens, Ambikā and Ambālikā. As a result, Dhṛtarāṣṭra and Pāṇḍu were born. The five Pāṇḍavas were born by following a similar method.

It seems that the practice was an acceptable solution of the paternity problem in the higher strata of society. But, evidently, it was a practice which was not held in high esteem. Kantawala calls it 'obnoxious'. There are indications in the text of the *Mahābhārata* itself as well as in the later *Dharmaśāstras*, which leave no doubt that this was not a usual custom.

Amiya Dev compares the war-and-peace effort of the Udyogaparvan with some Greek western parallels. He explicitly uses the term 'deconstruction', and so we may call his analysis a deconstruction of the episode. He rightly questions the sincerity of Kṛṣṇa in his peace efforts, as well as his alleged impartiality. He refers to the theophany of Kṛṣṇa when his peace mission failed, and raises some interesting points about its significance. On the whole the approach of Amiya Dev is that of a modern literary critic. The points raised by him are noteworthy.

In a very short paper, Kunjunni Raja refers to several episodes in the epic which gave rise to dilemmas. He views a moral dilemma as a situation where there are opposing pulls from strong moral values, such as truth and non-violence. He refers to the situation in the *Gītā*, which, he thinks, is a classic example of a conflict between individual duty and social responsibility.

Agrawal approaches the problem of Arjuna's moral predicament in the *Gītā* from the philosopher's point of view. He frequently refers to moral philosophers of modern times, and thereby illuminates the issues discussed in the *Gītā*. He depicts Arjuna as a moral agent who faces what may be called a classic example of a moral dilemma: to fight or not to fight. Obviously, neither the utilitarian ethic nor the Kantian ethic can resolve the conflict. Kṛṣṇa, however, suggested a way out which was not altogether ethical. According to Agrawal, Kṛṣṇa's answer can be understood at three levels: emotional, prudential, and ethical. Indeed, it provides an admixture of moral and non-moral reasons. Agrawal's analysis of Kṛṣṇa's response is very interesting.

Finally, Agrawal thinks that there is an ethical element in Kṛṣṇa's response; for, according to him, although moral dilemmas may appear to be unresolvable in our limited vision, they are resolvable when the knowledge of the ultimate order of the universe dawns upon us.

Kashap deals with a very controversial topic, namely, the concept of action in the *Gītā*. This topic has been much discussed by others, but Kashap concentrates upon a few verses, particularly of chapter four. He rightly emphasizes the profundity of the doctrine. He discusses the three related concepts: *karma, akarma* and *vikarma* where the second stands for 'inaction' or the state of actionlessness, and the third for wrong action. He gives an explanation of *niṣkāmakarma*. It refers to actions which are not prompted by such desires as are associated with emotions, for no action is possible without the promptings of some desire or other. Kashap refers to the importance which the *Gītā* places upon the notion of 'second order desire' (desire to have certain desires) for ethical purposes. This is an important philosophical insight of the *Gītā*.

In a scholarly paper, Y. Krishan discusses the implication of four key concepts: *dharma, artha, kāma*, and *mokṣa*. The *Mahābhārata* deals with all four of them, although it is primarily called the *Mokṣaśāstra*. Krishan quotes extensively from *Dharmaśāstra, Arthaśāstra*, and *Kāmaśāstra*. *Dharma* deals with ethics and religion, and *artha* is concerned with the creation of wealth and prosperity. *Kāma* means desire as well as sensuous enjoyment of life. Its goal is ultimately not pleasure but happiness. Now there are obvious conflicts among these three pursuits of life, but these conflicts are not unresolvable. In fact, the authors of the *śāstras* try to show how such conflicts are to be resolved. Hence these conflicts are to be separated from the cases of unresolvable moral dilemmas. Krishan points out how, in some places of the *Mahābhārata*, the poet describes that an amalgam of the three pursuits of life is possible.

BIMAL KRISHNA MATILAL

MORAL DILEMMAS: INSIGHTS FROM INDIAN EPICS

BIMAL KRISHNA MATILAL

INTRODUCTION

DILEMMAS are like paradoxes. Genuine paradoxes are seldom solved. They are, generally speaking, resolved or dissolved. Those philosophers and logicians, who have tried over the centuries to solve the well-known logical and semantical paradoxes, have more often than not created new problems elsewhere in the conceptual apparatus, which exposes the non-existence of a universally accepted solution. Paradoxes in other areas of knowledge have been more troublesome. Sometimes it has been conceded by people that paradoxes are what we learn to live with. Can moral dilemmas be put into the same category as those unsolvable paradoxes?

Theologians, ethicists and 'strong-minded' moral philosophers have often been reluctant to admit the reality of moral dilemmas; for if there can be genuine unsolvable moral dilemmas in a moral system, then it would be as good as courting defeat in our attempt to formulate rational moral theories. That is, it would be conceding inconsistency in a 'rational' moral system. It is assumed, therefore, that there must always be a right solution, a right path leading us out of the maze. Whether we can always find it or not, a solution exists. Moral dilemmas, on this view, are like ordinary mathematical puzzles, for which solutions are there, but we probably need a supermathematician to work them out.

It takes some courage to talk about moral dilemmas with regard to the great epic, the *Mahābhārata*. Indological scholars have often argued that Hindu orthodoxy would seldom agree that there are dilemmas in the teachings of the *Mahābhārata*. For is it not the case that Lord Kṛṣṇa is always in the *Mahābhārata* to play the role of the supermathematician and resolve the dilemmas for Arjuna? Is it not the case that Vidura is there to give the right kind of advice whenever the old, blind king Dhṛtarāṣṭra is in any dilemma, whether or not the blind king, being blind in more sense than one, pays any heed to the well-meaning and ever-righteous brother? Does not the deity Dharma, natural father of Yudhiṣṭhira, have to appear in many different forms—a mongoose, a stork, a yakṣa—and so on—in order to instruct and teach Yudhiṣṭhira the right path whenever dilemmas have presented themselves? It would be improbable to argue, on such a view, that there could have arisen any genuine dilemmas in the *dharma*-ethical system that has been delineated in the *Mahābhārata*.

One may further argue that no dilemmas were left dangling or unresolved except perhaps the unique case of Draupadī's question in Sabhāparvan. The situation can be unmistakably pin-pointed as the turning point of the entire story. It is uniquely described in the very beginning, the Ādiparvan, in Dhṛtarāṣṭra-Vilāpa:

> I did not hope for victory, O Sañjaya, when I heard poor Draupadī was dragged into the royal court with voice choked with tears wearing only a single piece of clothing. She had five husbands but still she was as if without any protector and hence publicly humiliated.

But the question that Draupadī asked was more concerned with the rights or legality of her husband's action than with the morality of the situation. Did Yudhiṣṭhira, having first lost his own freedom (as well as the freedom of the four brothers) and thus becoming a slave of the Kauravas, have any right to gamble again with Draupadī as the stake? The question reveals an intricate point of law or the legal convention of the community, and also makes a social point, the point of a social rebel, presumably of a non-conformist. In the story, the question was met by either silence or side-long glances. Bhīṣma, the oldest of the Kauravas, only recognized that this was 'a very good point'; but was unable to answer it. Only Vikarṇa, an insignificant character, sided with Draupadī. Society still did not allow the wife any freedom or autonomy as an independent person. It regarded wives as 'properties' of husbands, and hence can be staked in a gambling match. The incident seems to have a deep significance. If Draupadī's questions were properly answered, it would have required a 'paradigm shift' in India's social thought.

Both legal and social codes were designated by the pervasive term *dharma*, as were the moral principles or moral codes. The intentional ambiguity of the word *dharma*—its often-emphasized subtlety and ever-elusive nature (as Bhīṣma emphasized on this occasion)—is too well known to be mentioned here. Draupadī, on the other hand, was standing up for the rights and autonomy of the entire womanhood of that time, although she had to conform at the end, and the situation was saved by a miracle.

Let us take a close look at the dilemmas within the structure of the *dharma*-ethics as propounded in the epic. The main point, as I understand from the immense popularity and widespread discussion of such epic episodes, is to show that some of these moral dilemmas presented in the epic are illustrations of perennial problems in moral philosophy. Some of them have no satisfactory solution, although, in each case, an *ad hoc* practical action-guide was devised in the original story while the main problem remained unsolved. Over the ages we notice that these epic stories, various episodes, and subplots have been retold with great ingenuity in various regional and vernacular versions of the epics, in folk-tales, plays, dramas, etc. Each new version may be regarded as a novel attempt to resolve the dilemma inherent in the original version. In what follows, I shall concentrate particularly upon certain aspects of the *Mahābhārata*.

THE MAHĀBHĀRATA: ITS GREATNESS

I shall start with a remark V.S. Sukthankar made in 1942:[1] 'Whether we realize it or not, it remains a fact that we in India still stand under the spell of the *Mahābhārata*. There is many a strand that is woven in the thread of our civilization, reaching back into hoary antiquity.' In the same lecture series, posthumously published, he called this epic a 'dateless and deathless poem ... which forms the strongest link between India old and new.' After forty-five years, I do not think we can in any way challenge or differ from this great scholar of our country.

The *Mahābhārata* is a unique creation of India, one of its kind which has no equal in world literature. Thanks to the laudable efforts of Peter Brooks, the story, the underlying unique human drama, has been staged in cities like Paris, New York, and Glasgow in recent years with great success. Its popularity is no longer restricted to the geographical boundaries of India. This is the epic, which the well-known Indological scholars like Hermann Oldenberg[2] and E. Washbrook Hopkins[3] have called 'the most monstrous chaos' of an epic narrative, 'a text that is not a text'. It represents a corpus of some 200,000 lines, eight times the size of the *Illiad* and the *Odyssey* put together, that has influenced and captivated the minds of almost all Indians for about two millenia. The puzzlement of the older Indologists is understandable. Not only were the philological problems of their 'higher criticism' insuperable, and attempts to discover an *Ur-Mahābhārata* getting rid of everything else unsuccessful, but they seemed also to have seen the great paradoxes which this enormous text presents. It is, however, doubtful whether they really understood or enjoyed these paradoxes.

It suffices to say that, despite the untiring and life-long attempts of many worthy philologists and indologists, the 'epic nucleus' has never been discovered (unless we take the idiosyncratic solutions of some scholars at face value), for obviously a mere process of stripping off whatever one or the other scholar regards as interpolations cannot lead to a pure and unalloyed 'core' (peeling off onion-skins does not lead to any core, as we all know). Besides, why should there be only one 'core', and not a multitude of 'cores' or sources from which this multifaceted cultural epic might have developed? Search for the original epic nucleus, in this case, may very well be like the search for the original, virgin meaning of the text, which, according to some post-structuralist philosophers, did not exist in a unified way even at the origin.

For my purpose, I would take the *Mahābhārata* as a whole, the text that the critical edition has given us after the pruning away of a lot of unnecessary overgrowths. And I shall deal with the moral issues as treated in various episodes and sub-plots of the epic. I have taken some time to convince myself that the great epics, apart from being the source of everything else, constitute an important component of what we may term as moral philosophical thinking of the Indian tradition. Certainly, there exists a lacuna in the tradition of Indian philosophy. Professional philosophers of India over the last two thousand years have been consistently concerned with the problems of logic and epistemology, metaphysics and soteriology, and sometimes they have made very important contributions to the global heritage of philosophy. But, except some cursory comments and some insightful observations, the professional philosophers of India have very seldom discussed what we call moral philosophy today. It is true that the *Dharmaśāstra* texts were there to supplement the Hindu discussion of ethics, classification of virtues and vices, and enumeration of duties related to the social status of the individual. But morality was never discussed as such in these texts. On the other hand, the tradition itself was very self-conscious about moral values, moral conflicts and dilemmas, as well as about the difficulties of what we call practical reason or practical wisdom. This consciousness found its expression in the epic stories and narrative literature which can, therefore, be used for any illuminating discussion of moral philosophy in India. I propose to take this line of enquiry. The moral dilemmas presented in the *Mahābhārata* were in some sense universal, for most of them can be effectively used even today to illustrate arguments in moral philosophy.

Before I proceed any further I wish to make another point about my attitude towards the text of the *Mahābhārata*. Indologists have often distinguished between the narrative material and the didactic material in the epic. The implicit idea was that the didactic material was added to the narrative material and sometimes the narrative to the didactic, so that modern scholarship could separate one from the other. This seems to me a very artificial distinction as far as the text of the *Mahābhārata* is concerned. The so-called narrative and didactic material are found inextricably fused together in the text, such that they cannot be often differentiated. Sometimes the narrative itself imparts the moral lesson without any deliberate efforts on the part of the narrator. In other words, the medium itself is the message here.

WHAT IS A MORAL DILEMMA?

Let me first explain what I mean here by the term moral dilemma. A shallow critic might say: 'Well, since there was no concept of morality in Sanskrit, except "only a strict status compartmentalization of private and social ethics" (Max Weber),[4] how can there be moral dilemmas?' This was, however, not exactly the view of Max Weber. What I take here to be a view of the shallow critic can be regarded as a hypothetical construal of an opponent's view, a *pūrvapakṣa*. It is true, however, that morality is not an Indian term and its Sanskrit equivalent is not easy to find. The nearest that you can get is to use the rather ubiquitous and enigmatic term *dharma*. However, the basic assumption of the above question is wrong, for one cannot argue that, if a particular term was not used in a particular tradition, then the social or political reality denoted by the term would not also exist in that tradition. For, in that case, one might as well argue that, since the term 'religion' did not have a Sanskrit equivalent in ancient India, the social reality that you call religion did not exist in ancient or classical India.

Moral dilemmas are, in fact, very common in everyday life. Stories in classical and contemporary literature are full of such cases. Most moral dilemmas seem to remain unresolved in such stories. Very roughly, such dilemmas arise when the agent is committed to two or more moral obligations, but circumstances are such that an obligation to do *x* cannot be fulfilled without violating an obligation to do *y*. Dilemmas present irreconcilable alternatives, and the actual choice among them becomes either irrational or is based upon grounds other than moral. Moral philosophers have generally denied that such dilemmas are even possible, for an adequate moral theory is supposed to resolve such dilemmas; that is to say, it will show that such dilemmas are not genuine. In fact, today we may say that moral philosophers are divided into two camps: those who think that such dilemmas are not genuine and those, a tiny minority, who think that such dilemmas are both possible and actual.

Some ethicist-philosophers believe that there are probably ready-made recipes for avoiding conflicts in the moral domain. But the question is: whether such recipes are available when needed. There is no easy answer. Besides, weakness of the will plays an important role in the agent's final decision-making procedure. Can we think of two types of genuine dilemmas? In the case of one, what ought to be done has remained unsettled for the agent even when he has considered all the relevant information *known* to him in the situation. If we regard our weakness of will as incontinence *à la* Davidson, then we believe that, if the deemed informational constraint is removed, the dilemma will dissolve. But this is conceded to be only a matter of hope.

According to another type, what ought to be done remains unsettleable even after the exercise of all the rational means. Here, if the informational constraints are removed, it may not help the decision. Philosophical controversies have been more interesting when they arise around this second type of dilemma. My concern is primarily with the second type.

I personally believe that certain moral dilemmas are genuine, and also that occurrence of such dilemmas does not present any problem for moral realism. I shall not argue for these views here, but refer to other philosophers who have maintained such positions. My purpose here is to discuss certain striking and stimulating examples to be found in the great epics of India, specially in the *Mahābhārata*. My analysis will show that they were genuine dilemmas, and also that traditional wisdom, as I have emphasized, maintained an ambivalent attitude towards the *ad hoc* resolutions described in the ancient texts. Sometimes the same episodes were retold throughout the ages in plays, poems, and in different local versions of the epics. In these later versions, the *ad hoc* resolutions of the dilemmas were differently conceived, which probably reflects the changing pattern of the social ethos of the narrator's time.

A TYPICAL CASE IN THE EPIC

A typical case of moral dilemma is presented by Arjuna's question at the beginning of the *Bhagavadgītā*. Was Arjuna faced with a genuine moral dilemma? I shall come back to the question later on. Let us take another clear case of moral dilemma in an episode in the Karṇaparvan. Arjuna was faced with a choice between two irreconcilable obligations: promise-keeping and avoidance of fratricide. The incident that led to this is the following. On the very day of final encounter between Karṇa and Arjuna Yudhiṣṭhira fled the battlefield after being painfully humiliated by Karṇa in an armed engagement. When Arjuna came to the camp to pay visit to him and asked what really had happened, Yudhiṣthira flared up in anger and told Arjuna that all his boastfulness about being the finest archer in the world was a lot of nonsense, because the war was dragging on. He reminded Arjuna that the latter claimed to be capable of conquering everybody and thus end the war within a few days. In a rage, he not only insulted Arjuna but also slighted the 'Gāṇḍīva bow', the most precious possession of this valiant warrior. The bow was a gift to Arjuna from Agni, the fire-god. He held it so dear to his heart that he had promised to kill anyone who would ever speak ill of 'Gāṇḍīva'. Hence Yudhiṣṭhira's word put Arjuna in a very difficult situation: either he would have to kill his venerated elder brother or break his promise. When his Kṣatriya duty (*dharma*) made him choose the first alternative, Kṛṣṇa (his *alter ego*) appeared. On being asked Arjuna explained: he was obliged to commit fratricide in order to fulfil his obligation to keep his promise. Arjuna had full knowledge of the gravity of the crime he was about to commit but like a *mistimed* Kantian he had already taken a conflict-free decision to meet the Kṣatriya obligation of promise-keeping. A quotation from Kant's *Introduction to the Metaphysics of Morals* (1797) may be relevant here:[5]

> Because ... duty and obligation are in general concepts that express the objective practical necessity of certain actions and because two mutually opposing rules cannot be necessary at the same time, then if it is a duty to act according to one of them, it is not only not a duty but contrary to duty to act according to the other.

For Kant it seems that the objective practical rules should form a harmonious whole, a system characterized by consistency, much like a system of true beliefs. The moral conflict, which no doubt arises in the minds of the moral agents, cannot, therefore, be genuine. It would be at best a confusion, at worst an illusion. It conflates, according to Kant, a genuine duty with a *ground* of that duty. Hence, in a so-called dilemma, one horn is a genuine duty, and the other is merely a ground of duty. There may be conflict between grounds but not between duties. Hence, in Kantian ethics, no agent can be forced to violate his duty. This is at least one of the interpretations of Kantian thought. Hence Arjuna might be said to be anticipating the Kantian model.

Kṛṣṇa, however, was not Kant. When he intercepted and started a discourse with Arjuna, he obviously turned an apparently moral conflict into a genuine moral dilemma. Promise-keeping is, indeed, a strong obligation. Plato is supposed to have described a typical case of dilemma, in which the return of a cache of arms has been promised to a man who, intent on starting mayhem, comes to claim them. Conflict was generated here by two opposing principles, that of promise-keeping and that of benevolence.[6] In fact, promise-keeping is regarded as equivalent to truth-telling. In Sanskrit, promise-keeping is sometimes classed as 'protecting the truth' (*satya-rakṣā*). Hence, both in India and the West, the two obligations are invariably connected. There is no cultural relativism here. In Kantian ethics, truth-telling gets the highest priority. Kṛṣṇa, however, continued to argue that promise-keeping or even truth-telling cannot be an unconditional obligation when it is in conflict with the avoidance of grossly unjust and criminal acts such as patricide or fratricide. Saving an innocent life is also a strong obligation, saving the life of an elder brother would naturally be an equally strong obligation, if not stronger. Hence, in fact, according to Kṛṣṇa, two almost equally strong obligations or duties are in conflict here.

KṚṢṆA'S STORY TO SUPPORT HIS ARGUMENT

Kṛṣṇa related a story to illustrate his point. A hermit, Kauśika by name, once took a vow of telling the truth throughout his life. One day he faced the following dilemma. Some bandits were chasing several travellers with the intention of killing them. Kauśika was sitting nearby at the crossroad. The traveller passed by, and requested him not to show the miscreants which way they had fled. Kauśika did not answer. Soon the bandits arrived, and, knowing that the hermit would not lie, asked him about the travellers; and Kauśika told the truth. As a result, the travellers were caught and killed. Kṛṣṇa added that Kauśika did not reach heaven after his death (his much-coveted reward) just because of this act of cruelty. Although he abided by his principle of truth-telling throughout his life, it came to no effect. The major point was that, under situational constraints, there might be stronger grounds for rejecting truth-telling as a duty and accepting the stronger duty of saving an innocent life. This encapsulates a very strong moral insight, although it is not Kantian.

For Kṛṣṇa *dharma* is at least sometimes dictated by the constraints or the contingency of the situation (*Āvasthika*, *Mahābhārata*, xii, 36.2). But this is no defence of opportunism. Truth-telling has been extolled as one of the highest virtues in the tradition. We should not have any illusion, despite frequent criticisms to the contrary that the tradition of the *Dharmaśāstras* or the religious texts of India underplayed the importance of truth-telling as a virtue and a value. Āpastaṃbha says plainly that every perjurer goes to hell. Thus, there does not seem to be any religious, textual or *Dharmaśāstric* support for sweeping comments such as 'all Hindoos are compulsive liars' (Lord Curzon). But it must be admitted that excusable untruths were permitted by such writers of *Dharmaśāstras* as Gautama and Manu. Thus, perjury to save life was permitted as a *dharma*. Hence Kṛṣṇa's story is compatible with the general dictum of *Dharmaśāstras* (*dharma*-ethics).

KṚṢṆA AND R.M. HARE

There are several intricate issues of moral philosophy that can be discussed here in connection with this epic story. There are those philosophers, who admit the factuality of moral dilemmas and insist that our commitment to consistency would require us to modify the system by reordering priorities or by discarding certain principles. For example, R.M. Hare believes that our moral precepts, 'do not lie', can be reformulated in the light of wartime experience as 'do not lie except to the enemy in time of war', which will be the more adequate principle and make the system consistent by resolving a conflict situation.[7] Alternatively, moral conflicts can be resolved with a 'higher' type of critical thinking. Hare has distinguished between two types of cases: the intuitive perception or the intuitive level of thinking done by one whom he calls 'the prole', and the critical level of thinking done by a more exemplary figure whom he calls 'the Archangel'. Oddly enough, this may just fit the episode described in the *Mahābhārata*. It is tempting to say that Arjuna was acting like 'the Prole', while Kṛṣṇa intervened and became 'the Archangel' of Hare. Hare's system acknowledges progressive revision of our moral principles in the light of conflict situations that are bound to arise. It may be suitable to some extent to regard Kṛṣṇa as an anachronistic exemplar of the Harean model. But I believe the problems we face at various stages of the epic are much deeper than what would fit such simpler explanations.

KṚṢṆA AND SARTRE

Jean-Paul Sartre gives a striking example of practical conflict where a young man must choose between his patriotic duty to join the French Resistance and his filial obligation to care for his aging mother.[8] Sartre, like Hare, acknowledges the reality of this conflict, but uses such *hard* cases as evidence to draw the conclusion that it is useless for a moral agent to form an ordered system of ethical principles and to try to live by it. The agent, according to Sartre, is *condemned to be free*. Sartre takes man to be *condemned*, because 'he did not create himself'; yet he is *free*, because 'from the moment that he is thrown into this world he is responsible for everything he does'. He, therefore, should use his radical liberty, and improvise his choice according to the situation without regret or remorse. In the *Mahābhārata* episode, we again see a resonance of the Sartrean advice in Kṛṣṇa's advice to Arjuna. Kṛṣṇa said to Arjuna after relating the story of Kauśika that Arjuna, unlike Kauśika, must not regret his failure to keep the promise when the concrete situation would otherwise require him to commit fratricide. Again, in the *Gītā* a Sartrean reading of Kṛṣṇa is possible, but perhaps we should avoid the temptation. The situation is comparable in respect of the recommendation of the unregretted choice to be reached (*māsucaḥ*) but not so, as far as the complete rejection of the search for a consistent ethical system is concerned. Kṛṣṇa also would not say that humans are *condemned* to be free. Sartre's example has been much discussed by others. Sartre himself says that the agent is 'hesitating between two kinds of morality' (*Speech Act*, p. 296), which neither Christian doctrine nor Kantian ethics can help him resolve.

SUBTLETY OF DHARMA-ETHICS: DHARMA AND LUCK

Let us discuss some details of the *Mahābhārata* episode. Kṛṣṇa emphasized the fact that it is very difficult but not impossible to understand the extremely subtle ways of *dharma* or duty (*dharmāṇāṁ gatiṃ śūkṣmaṁ duranvayam*).[9] He also said that even Bhīṣma or Vidura or Kuntī would have been able to resolve the dilemma for Arjuna. To sum up Kṛṣṇa's argument:

> It is true that truth-telling is the highest virtue but there are mitigating circumstances such as destruction of the innocent lives and loss of all possessions under which to tell a lie may be a duty ('where telling a lie may be as good as "truth" and truth-telling may be as good as lying').[10]

Before telling the story of Kauśika, Kṛṣṇa, told another story about an innocent hunter called Balāka. Balāka used to hunt animals to feed his blind parents. He was innocent and simple-hearted. But he had a rare skill. He could hunt an animal even when it was outside the range of his sight, simply by listening to the noise made by the animal drinking water from a river. One day, by chance, he hunted, in this manner, a ferocious creature called Andha. But, as soon as Andha was killed, gods showered flowers from heaven, and the celestial chariot came to fetch Balāka to heaven. Why? For Balāka unknowingly did a great service to the lord's creation, because this Andha had grown up to be a terrible creature who was almost unkillable. Having received a boon from Lord Brahmā, he went on killing all the creatures. He was in a way out to destroy all creatures. Although Balāka was unaware of this fact, he was somehow able to kill this evil creature, and thereby obtained his just reward. This story sounds like the case of 'moral luck'. The goodness of a good human life is not always dependent on the things that the moral agent can control. There is 'external contingency' or luck coming to the agent from the world which is not under his control. But this contingency cannot be totally eliminated. Sometimes such contingencies would generate moral dilemmas, for the agent. Balāka was a good person in his own modest way, but external contingencies made his moral reward far greater than what he had dreamt of. By contrast Kauśika had a project for life which included the covetable moral reward, heaven, but external contingencies intervened and Kauśika was faced with a situation in which he was forced to act. But, according to Kṛṣṇa's ethical system, he acted stupidly, and chose the alternative that ruined his dream totally. Kṛṣṇa said that, although Kauśika wanted to do his duty (*dharmakāmaḥ*), he was unwise (*apaṇḍita*) and a fool (*mūḍha*, *Mahābhārata*, 8.49.32).

TYPES OF CONFLICT: MORAL AND NON-MORAL

We have to discuss a whole spectrum of cases where some conflict of duties invariably arises, but, as we all know, some conflicts are more serious than others, for not all conflicts of duties can be raised to the status of a moral dilemma. Let us note four types of cases where conflict arises. In all cases, the agent wants to do *x* as well as *y*; but, since both cannot be done because of contingencies of circumstances, he does *x* and foregoes *y*.

CASE 1: What is foregone, i.e. *y*, is a reward or a possession.
CASE 2: *y* may be simply an omission or failure to pursue a desired project. (Let us note two subvarieties, at least.)
CASE 2*a*: When the desired project is not central to the agent's final commitment in life, i.e. it is a luxury.
CASE 2*b*: When the desired project is central to the agent's final commitment in life.
CASE 3: When *y* is something that, if it is not done, the omission is harmful. Two subvarieties again.
CASE 3*a*: When it is harmful to the agent.
CASE 3*b*: When it is harmful to others.
CASE 4: When non-doing of *y* does harm to the agent or to others, but is reparable.

Both epics, the *Rāmāyaṇa* and the *Mahābhārata*, are full of episodes which would present conflict situations of one or the other kind. The above list is not exhaustive.[11] However, it can help our discussion of the Kauśika incident as well as the dilemma that was faced by Arjuna. Was Kauśika faced with a real moral dilemma? I believe opinions will vary. If Kauśika belonged to our case 1, one would hardly think that it was a moral dilemma. In fact, one would say that it should have been more moral for him to save the lives of others even by foregoing his reward in heaven. This would be similar to the case where the captain of the ship throws his valuable cargo into the ocean in order to save the lives of the passengers.

How about case 2? Kauśika may properly belong here. He had a life-plan, a project that was central to his life. So his case would be similar to case 2*b*, for truth-telling was central to his life-plan.

Would he then be justified in foregoing this duty so central to his life-plan, and tell a lie to save travellers? Is this what Kṛṣṇa's ethics demanded? It is not difficult to see, in this case, that Kauśika had a genuine dilemma, and that that dilemma was moral. If truth-telling was only peripheral to Kauśika's life-plan, i.e. if he belonged to our case 2*a*, then, of course, one could easily say that Kauśika chose the wrong alternative from a moral point of view. But case 2*b* makes the conflict more evenly balanced. Hence a theory of ranking the alternative becomes necessary. Kṛṣṇa's ethics demanded such ordering of priorities. It was said by Kṛṣṇa that, according to him, saving the lives of the creatures should get the highest priority (*prāṇinām avadhas tāta sarvajyāyān mato mama*, *Mahābhārata*, 8.249.20 cr. ed.). He clearly ranked the value of saving a life higher than telling the truth. Here Kṛṣṇa clearly deviated from Kant, or even from the ideal that sometimes was upheld by Rāma in the *Rāmāyaṇa*. In other words, anachronistically speaking, Rāma was more Kantian. But I believe Kṛṣṇa's ethics had concern for a richer scheme of values, moral or non-moral, presupposing a very complex societal and familial structure. It also envisions a society when saving innocent lives has a higher priority.

KṚṢṆA AND KANT

When Kant asserted that truth-telling should unconditionally get the highest priority, it is interesting to note that an example was cited which was similar to the Kauśika story of Kṛṣṇa. A contemporary French philosopher criticized it and said that, if a murderer had been chasing a person who had taken shelter in the house of a moral agent, it would not be the obligation of the agent to tell the truth to the murderer. Kant, in reply,[12] argued that truth-telling would be an unconditional obligation, and, therefore, the contingency of the situation should not affect it at all. Kant, however, made some comments in the appendix of his *Critique of Practical Reason* which are worth mentioning. Kant argued that truth-telling, in that case, would not necessarily lead to the murder. For it might not have been easy for the murderer to locate the person who was hiding. Or the victim might have fled by the back door. Or, when the murderer would be searching for the victim, the police or other neighbours might rush in as a group to stop the murderer and arrest him. These remarks of Kant are of interest to us, for they show that even a great philosopher like Kant was trying to find a way out of the tight corner which had arisen as the combined result of his rigid ethical principle and sound logical reason.

Our case 3*a* would also be easily decidable, if we believed in the notion of morality that is concerned with other-regarding actions. For example, Kauśika had actually four choices open to him. He could (*i*) tell a lie, (*ii*) remain silent, (*iii*) courageously tell the bandits that he would not help them; and (*iv*) tell the truth (which he did). He would have saved an innocent life, if he followed anyone of the first three choices. By lying he would have to accept some harm coming to him, i.e. moral culpability. But he had desired for heaven. Hence this adherence to truth may not be a genuine moral stance. For, according to some philosophers today, the moral claim is a claim that cannot be avoided even by eliminating desires.[13] If he had eliminated his desire for heaven, he would have lied to save innocent lives, for that would then have been his *moral* obligation.

The second or the third choice would have been more risky, but they were morally more attractive, for a great deal of moral courage would have been necessary. The Davidsonian idea of weakness of the will as 'incontinence' might supply a relevant point here. The bandits might have tortured the hermit, if he remained silent or explicitly refused to tell them the truth. Kṛṣṇa himself refers to such alternatives. He says that, if, under such circumstances, one could get away by remaining silent,[14] one should remain silent. But if one saw that one could not remain silent, it would be better for one to lie and mislead the miscreants.[15] The third choice, however, seems to be morally the most attractive one. But this also takes account of the moral character of the agent himself. A person must be ready to accept inhuman torture to save the lives of others. This would have pleased a Kantian. The Kantian ethic says that we must never regard another person as a means but always as an end. Hence it would have been difficult to see how by telling the truth Kauśika avoided treating the travellers as means. For the same reason, it is difficult to see how truth-telling as a duty can never be subject to external contingency.

KṚṢṆA'S RESOLUTION: REMORSE AND REGRET

If Kauśika had chosen the third way, he could have been tortured to death by the bandits. But this would have been at least a moral victory. Giving up one's life to save the lives of others was also regarded as the highest virtue in the epic tradition of India, as other epic episodes such as that of Dadhīci would clearly show.

Case 4 needs some further comments. It seems to be particularly relevant to our epic story where breaking a promise may be *reparable*. It is somewhat amusing to note that, when Arjuna was not only regretful but also remorseful, having foregone his obligation for truth-keeping or promise-keeping, Kṛṣṇa suggested that this omission was reparable. When Arjuna promised to *kill* the person who would insult his Gāṇḍīva bow, he was obviously not thinking of Yudhiṣṭhira as his victim. Now, since Yudhiṣṭhira was the intended victim who was also his revered elder brother, he could even keep his promise without actually killing him physically. Since insult and harsh words to such an elder brother would be as good as killing him in spirit, Arjuna could now insult Yudhiṣṭhira and use harsh words, and thus keep his promise. This type of 'face-saving' solution was suggested by Kṛṣṇa and accepted by Arjuna. A childish solution to the problem posed by a childish sort of promise! But I do not think the semantic issue raised by Kṛṣṇa can be totally ignored, even when he acknowledged its levity; for a promise-maker has to articulate his promise in the sentence of some natural language, where the relevant semantic rules must apply. And, according to a prevailing philosophical view, the intention of the speaker is also a factor for determining the meaning of a sentence.[16] Apart from the levity, we must note also that truth-keeping was not given up as a moral obligation for a person like Arjuna. I believe the dilemma has not been trivialized here. The moral agent's sentiment as well as his commitment have rather been respected. What was recoverable is salvaged from the conflict.

According to modern philosophers, genuine moral dilemmas generate what may be called the 'tragic cases' which are characterized by remorse or guilt which the agents experience after having acted in conflict situations. This feeling of *guilt* must be genuine, and it must be distinguished from the feeling of simple *regret*. We have seen that those who want to deny the reality of moral dilemmas would deny such moral sentiments on the part of moral agents. But, in the case of genuine dilemma, the agent, while doing x would be invariably overwhelmed with a feeling of remorse for not doing y. Hence, in a moral system, which acknowledges moral dilemmas, such moral sentiments are unavoidable, and neither of the conflicting obligations is permanently given up. The obligation that is overridden is only rendered temporarily ineffectual by the constraints of the particular situation. Arjuna had his share of remorse both in the beginning of the battle of Kurukṣetra and here. Hence the system that is outlined here makes room for genuine moral dilemmas with the attendant moral sentiments, remorse, regret, etc. as I have tried to show above. Hence I believe there was a genuine moral dilemma at the beginning of the *Gītā* with which Arjuna was confronted. But this is not the place to enter into this issue.

CONCLUSION

The nature of our practical wisdom has a sort of malleability, which is comparable to the ever-elusive nature of *dharma*-ethics to be found in our epic literature. It has been said that *dharmasya tatvaṃ nihitaṃ guhāyām* (the truth of *dharma* lies in the dark cave). It cannot be completely known by us as universally fixed. But the acknowledgement of possible flexibility does not mean that the fixity and universality of ethical laws will be entirely negotiable. Situational constraints may require some bending, but by allowing genuine moral sentiments like remorse or guilt it makes up for occasional lapses. A moral agent exercises his practical wisdom, and also learns from the experiences he passes through during his life. He has an *enriched* practical wisdom when it is informed by his experiences of genuine moral dilemmas. A moral agent needs also a character which is nothing but a disposition to act and react appropriately with moral concerns. His later desires would be informed by the experiences he passes through, and he would, therefore, react appropriately when confronted with further moral dilemmas. This is the kind of moral insight that can be derived from a scrutiny of the Kṛṣṇa-ethics in the *Mahābhārata*.

In our review of the history of moral thought of mankind as a whole, we usually come across two different types of moral persons as paradigmatic. One is the dutiful fulfiller of universal obligations *à la* Kant. In India, we have Rāma whose moral ideals would fall into this category. The nature of *dharma* idealized by Rāma (or Yudhiṣṭhira) seems to have been very rigid. It seldom bends. The other paradigmatic person we meet in the moral field can be described as an imaginative poet. He becomes a perspectivist and understands the contingency of the human situation. He realizes the necessity of 'paradigm shifts' much like the revolutionary scientists in Thomas Kuhn's description of the nature of scientific revolutions.[17] He looks at the particularity of the situation but also looks beyond it. He is our Kṛṣṇa. So Kṛṣṇa allows for flexibility in *dharma*. But this flexibility never means the 'anything goes' kind of morality. He is the *poet* who accepts the constraints of metres, verses, and metaphors. But he is also the strong poet who has absolute control over them. He uses metres, verses, and metaphors to produce the music which you cannot but admire. He governs from above but does not dictate.

It is interesting to note that, towards the end of the nineteenth century, there was an important dispute on this very issue between Bankimchandra Chatterjee and Rabindranath Tagore wherein Bankimchandra supported the ethics of Kṛṣṇa and commented that truth-telling cannot be an unconditional value. Young Rabindranath, however, protested and said that this only showed how devious a follower of Kṛṣṇa would have to be. The arguments and counter-arguments of these two stalwarts rolled on for a while in the pages of the contemporary Bengali periodicals. It was young Rabindranath who somewhat unconsciously supported a Kantian moral stance. Both agreed that the third alternative (Kauśika saying, 'I know but I'll not tell you') would have been the best. A few years later, another story was reported in the gossip column of a Calcutta newspaper which concerned another famous man, a professor belonging to the Brahmo Samāj, Heramba Maitra. Apparently, he was asked by a traveller about the location of the Star Theatre. But since he morally disapproved of what went on in the Star Theatre, his first reaction was to say that he did not know. When he realized that this was a lie, he came back, called the traveller and told him: 'Look, I know where the Star Theatre is but I will not tell you'. All this shows how concerned our present-day moral thinking still is with the dilemmas presented in the traditional epics.

NOTES

1. V.S. Sukthankar, *On the Meaning of the Mahābhārata*, p. 32.
2. Herman Oldenberg, *Die Literatur Des Alten Indien*, Stuttgart and Berlin, 1903.
3. E. Washbrook Hopkins, *The Great Epic of India*, 1901.
4. Max Weber, *Wirtschaft und Gesellschaft*, Colonge and Berlin, 1964, 1:366.
5. Immanuel Kant, *Introduction to the Metaphysics of Morals*, academi ed., p. 293.
6. See R.B. Marcus, 'Moral Dilemma and Consistency' in *Journal of Philosophy*, 77 (198), pp. 121-36.
7. R.M. Hare, *The Language of Morals*, p. 50.
8. J.P. Sartre, *L'Existentialisme est un humanisme*. My reference is from Walfer Kaufman, *Existentialism*, p. 295.
9. The *Mahābhārata* (cr. ed.), 8.49.28.
10. *Ibid.*, 8.49.29.
11. Most of these varieties are noted in Martha Nussbaum's *The Fragility of Goodness*, pp. 27-50. In what follows I have derived several points from her book to illuminate my discussion and analysis of the Indian epic stories.
12. See Immanuel Kant, *Critique of Practical Reuson* (Abbott's translation), appendix pp. 361-63.
13. See B. Williams, *Self*, 1973; 166-86.
14. *The Mahābhārata*, 8.49.51.
15. *Ibid.*, 8.49.52.
16. In many ordinary situations in our life we use the word 'kill' loosely in a wider sense: For example, a mother may tell the child 'if you do this, I will kill you'. This, of course, leads to the problem of literal versus metaphorical uses of the word—an intricate issue which I do not wish to enter into here. This may also not be relevant to the context.
17. For a clear notion of 'paradigm shifts', see Thomas Kuhn. However, I am using the term in an extended sense.

MORAL DILEMMAS IN THE MAHĀBHĀRATA

T. S. RUKMANI

THE *Mahābhārata* describes itself as a *dharmaśāstra*, an *arthśāstra*, a *kāmaśāstra*, and a *mokṣaśāstra*,[1] and then goes on to proclaim that whatever is here in this book may be found elsewhere, but what is not found here cannot be found anywhere else.[2] Though the corc of the *Mahābhārata* story could have existed before Pāṇini as P.V. Kane says in his *History of Dharmaśāstras*,[3] it is well known that the *Mahābhārata* took a long time to reach its present size.[4] Unlike the *Rāmāyaṇa* wherein Vālmīki has woven a well-knit story round the characters of Rāma and Sītā, the *Mahābhārata* can at best keep the thread of the main event intact, while the other events and stories are just fitted in as and when they arise without being directly connected with the main narrative of the epic.

When one then talks of the 'moral dilemmas' in such a work, one has to start with a clear idea as to what exactly one is looking for. The first assumption then is that there is a standard moral behaviour against which one measures the deviations which then give rise to the dilemma problem. Moreover, both in a moral dilemma and in a moral conflict there is a deep mental struggle involved, and a definite line of demarcation between the two is difficult to achieve. Therefore, an attempt on those lines has not been the aim of this paper.

To word it differently, if *dharma* consists in always telling the truth, then will telling a lie in order to save someone who would be killed if the truth be told be *adharma*.[5] This can be one kind of 'moral dilemma'. But a 'moral dilemma' can also arise when there are two courses of action—*A* and *B*—which entail the same result, but where action *A* may be considered to be more moral than action *B*.

Let us take the case of Yudhiṣṭhira. He was coaxed into telling a lie in order to unnerve Droṇācārya. He agreed to the deceit, but quietened his conscience by uttering a lie coated as truth. He knew that he was deceiving Droṇa; and, by dressing it up to mean the death of an elephant called Aśvatthāma, he ultimately distorted the very meaning of morality. Since morality is ultimately concerned with a mental framework of doing what is right and not just with verbal correctness, Dharmaputra was guilty of an immoral act when he uttered loudly within the hearing of Droṇa 'Aśvatthāma is dead', and added softly 'whether the man or the elephant'.[6] However, this paper will concentrate on the moral dilemma of the first kind, i.e. where the behaviour will be assessed against an expected moral standard.

The first assumption in this exercise, then, is that there is a standard moral behaviour. Unless this assumption is made, the utterances of a number of characters in the *Mahābhārata* cannot be understood. Let us look at that famous speech by Duryodhana in the Gadāparvan where he nearly summarizes the various misdeeds of the Pāṇḍavas and Kṛṣṇa, or the breaking of *dharma* by Kṛṣṇa and the Pāṇḍavas in the Kurukṣetra battle. Addressing Kṛṣṇa he says:

> Wretch, son of a slave, was not your father Vasudeva, Kaṃsa's slave? You speak like a shameless wretch. I saw you instigate Bhīma to aim his blow at my thigh. Do you think I did not see you making as though casually talking to Arjuna pointing at your thigh but really indicating to Bhīma that he should strike me on the thighs disregarding the laws of single combat? Till then, it was an equal battle. You have neither pity nor shame. Did you not contrive the death of grandsire Bhīṣma through cunning? You advised Śikhaṇḍin to be placed in front when attacking Bhīṣma, knowing that the grandsire would scorn to fight a woman and would let himself be mortally wounded without resistance. You brought about the end of Droṇācārya through making Dharmaputra utter a falsehood. You were the father of that deadly lie that issued from Yudhiṣṭhira's mouth and made Droṇa throw his bow away. Did you not look on

without protest and rejoice when that wretch Dhṛṣṭadyumna attacked and killed the *ācārya* who had stopped fighting, throwing away his weapons and settling down in a *yoga* posture for meditation on the Supreme? Was it not you who wickedly contrived to make Karṇa hurl the fatal spear at Ghaṭotkaca instead of reserving it for Arjuna as he had all along resolved to do? O great sinner, surely it was you who instigated Sātyaki to butcher Bhūriśravas when his right arm had been foully cut off and he stopped fighting and spread his arrows for a seat for meditation. It was you who brought about the death of Karṇa by inducing Arjuna to attack him in a cowardly manner when he was engaged in lifting his chariot wheel which had sunk and stuck in the mud in the field of battle. O worthless man, sole cause of our destruction, the whole world has condemned your act when by sorcery you made it appear as if the sun had set to make Jayadratha, the Sindhu king, to believe that the day was over and he was past danger and then you caused him to be slain when he was off his guard.'[7]

It is the same assumption which startles Yudhiṣṭhira in the Svargārohaṇaparvan, when seeing Duryodhana in *svarga* he questions the justification of such a one as Duryodhana who is *adharma* incarnate attaining *svarga*.[8]

We also have numerous statements like: 'Victory is where *dharma* is.'[9] '*Dharma* is eternal whereas pleasure and pain are not.'[10] It is, thus, clear that in the above statements everything is weighed and evaluated against a standard *dharma*.

Our next question would then naturally be whether there is a '*standard dharma*'. While the answer to that is in the affirmative, it is when one starts defining it that one gets into various difficulties. But one can say that moral standards in the Indian tradition, right from Vedic times, were intuitively grasped to be self-evident. In the *Ṛgveda*, at least, a moral principle is something acceptable, because it has a sense of value. In order to understand this, it is necessary to look briefly at *dharma* in the *Ṛgveda* and then trace its growth in various forms till its culmination in the many-branched tree of the *Mahābhārata*.

In the *Ṛgveda*, *dharma* is used both as an adjective and as a noun, meaning both 'religious rites' and the 'one that nourishes or sustains'.[11] But *dharma* is generally confined to the religious sphere at this stage of its conception. Its different meanings as given in the *Taittirīyopaniṣad* and other Upaniṣads,[12] seem to have developed by combining the idea of *dharma* with that of *ṛta* in the *Ṛgveda*. While *dharma* had connection with the individual, his actions, his obligations, etc. *ṛta* stood for a cosmic order by which the various phenomena in nature follows a prescribed course. *Ṛta* is thus a cosmic force, and even the gods are subject to its laws.[13] *Ṛta* also stood for moral order, and the god Varuṇa is the dispenser of the fruits of the man who follows the truth.[14] Thus, a whole range of moral and physical harmony came to be associated with *ṛta*. Since *dharma* also evolved along the same lines, when *ṛta* went out of usage *dharma* took on a number of meanings like custom, moral laws, laws, duties in general, what is right; in short, 'the principle that holds together the whole universe, physical as well as moral.'[15] *Dharma* is the 'ideal in conduct towards which we must move in order to perfect ourselves spiritually.'[16]

While the development of *dharma* took on many forms in later times, what is significant during its entire growth is that it clung on to its *ṛta* component throughout its entire growth. *Dharma* could be interpreted differently with reference to various social institutions and different situations in an individual's life. But when it stood for the *ṛta* component, it stood for morality *per se*. *Ṛta* was not concerned with what was right conventionally or the rightness of which can often be understood only with reference to the tradition of a particular community; it was concerned with general moral principles. These were acceptable, because they were intuitively grasped and they satisfied the sense of value in a rational being. It is the *ṛta* aspect which lent *dharma* its mystical quality, and it stood for the ideal in the conduct of man. As society grew and expanded, *dharma* also had to accommodate itself to the changes in society. Thus, there evolved various *dharma* like *varṇadharma*, *āśramadharma*, *kuladharma*, *deśadharma*, *kāladharma*, and so on. The resilience of the Indian ethos to absorb new groups of people and institutions and fit them into various categories of *dharmas* is evident at this stags. It is generally said that, if there had been only the various classes and castes without the overriding concept of *dharma*, ancient Indian civilization would also have met the same fate as other ancient civilizations like the Sumerian, Egyptian, etc. Since *dharma* was also sacred and had divine sanction, it became part of religion and philosophy as *adṛṣṭa* or *puṇya* and *pāpa,* so much so that in one philosophy at least *dharma* usurped the place of god and gained paramount, importance. *Dharma* in religion and philosophy is concerned with the *ṛta* aspect, even though sometimes restricted in scope as in the *Pūrvamimāṃsā* school. In religion and philosophy the aim of *dharma* is liberation. Thus, the *Vaiśeṣikasūtras* mention that *dharma* is that which achieves *abhyudaya* and *niḥśreyaḥ*.[17]

Dharma took on another mantle when it became part of religion and philosophy. Since the *ātman* is a permanent entity, what we call life is a happening to work out the results of *adṛṣṭa* or *dharma* and *adharma*; and *dharma* is thus closely connected with the doctrine of *karma*. In its early history, though *karma* was connected with religious rites or rituals, thus connecting it directly with *dharma* in the sense of religious rites, in the Vedas (*Ṛgveda*) *karma* gradually expanded its meaning to include any kind of action which will sooner or later yield its result, if not in this life then in any one of the series of lives that one will obtain. And this gradually came to mean whatever was destined to be. In this way *dharma, karma* and *bhoga* (or experience) are closely connected. It is this interconnectedness which stands out clearly when one studies the *Mahābhārata*.

The story of Karṇa in the *Mahābhārata* brings out this connection very clearly.[18] Karṇa learnt archery from Paraśurāma under the pretext that he was a Brāhmaṇa, as Paraśurāma would not have taught him otherwise. While Karṇa was practising with his bow one day in the forest, a Brāhmana's cow was accidentally hit and killed. The Brāhmaṇa then cursed Karṇa saying: 'In battle your chariot wheel will get stuck in the mud, and you will be done to death even like this innocent cow which you have killed.' This is because killing a cow is prohibited, according to the *Dharmasūtras*.[19] Paraśurāma one day fell asleep on Karṇa's lap. An insect bit Karṇa very badly on the thigh, but Karṇa bore the pain and did not move for fear of waking up his guru. But the warm blood trickling from the wound woke up Paraśurāma, and he at once shouted: 'You are a kṣatriya, otherwise you could not have borne this physical pain without stirring. You are not a

Brāhmaṇa. You have deceived your teacher. When your hour comes, your knowledge of the *astras* will fail you, and what you have learnt from me through deception will not be useful to you.'[20] Even the insect which bore into Karṇa's thigh was an Asura in a previous birth condemned to be born as an insect till released from the curse in the manner stated.

Karṇa was invincible as long as he had the divine ear-rings and armour with which he was born. Therefore, Indra, the father of Arjuna, came in the garb of a Brāhmaṇa, and begged Karṇa to present him with his ear-rings and armour which he did. Karṇa had also promised Kuntī that he would kill only one of the Pāṇḍavas, when she went to plead with him to change sides, as he was the eldest of her sons.

Thus, the *Mahābhārata* depicts the end of Karṇa as one that was destined to happen.

As the goal set for itself is encyclopaedic, the *Mahābhārata* continued the Vedic tradition by interpreting and reinterpreting the legends and incidents in the light of changes that were taking place in society. It is thus a fine study in hermeneutics. For instance, in the Dakṣa legend described in the *Śatapatha Brāhmaṇa* and the *Kauśītakī Brāhmaṇa*, the exclusion of Rudra from Dakṣa's sacrifice and the cause for Rudra's destruction of the sacrifice are quite different. The reason given there is that Prajāpati Dakṣa had intercourse with his daughter Uṣa and to remedy the evil effects of this the gods created a new being called Bhūtavān (perhaps Rudra) who was commanded to pierce Prajāpati. In the Veda, there is no reference to Rudra's marriage with Dakṣa's daughter.[21] But in the *Śāntiparva* of the *Mahābhārata*, there are two versions of the same story given. One agrees more or less with the puraṇic version of the legend, while the other proclaims the greatness of Rudra.

Traditionally, the epics are considered to explain further what is contained in the Vedas.[22] This, combined with its own claim of containing everything within itself, makes it clear that the author or authors of the *Mahābhārata*, at various periods, tried to reinterpret the stories and legends in keeping with the social and religious climate of the time. Thus, the offence committed by Dakṣa for which Rudra caused the destruction of the sacrifice is his intercourse with his daughter Uṣa, and there is no reference to Rudra's marrige with Dakṣa's daughter in the Vedas. So also the person who destroyed the sacrifice was created by the gods and was called Bhūtavān. This story took on various forms in keeping with the changing notion of *dharma*, both in the religious and in the social sense. The identification of Rudra and Śiva was already accomplished by this time, and the rules of endogamy and exogamy were already laid down by the various *Dharmasūtras*. *Niyoga* was an accepted social custom, and was part of the Kṣatriyadharma from ancient times. But its acceptance varied from age to age. While Gautama, Bauddhāyana, Viṣṇu and Vasiṣṭha allow *niyoga*, Āpastaṃba condemns it.[23] Again, Manu allows *niyoga* in one place,[24] while condemning it at another place.[25] But Yājñavalkya, who is considered later, does not condemn *niyoga*.[26] Kauṭilya allows *niyoga* even in the case of Brahmaṇas.[27] The *Mahābhārata* fully approves of *niyoga* and allows its wide practice. But the *Smṛtisāṃgraha* prohibits *niyoga* in the Kali age.[28] It is this change in *dharma* which makes the *Mahābhārata* try to explain away Draupadī's marrying the five Pāṇḍavas. So also Bhīma's drinking warm blood from the throat of Duḥśāsana is explained as if Bhīma was only feigning to do so.[29]

Dharma by its very nature cannot be static. When the basis of *dharma* is discussed, especially when there is a doubt, Manu states that the sources of *dharma* are the Vedas, Smṛtis, character, conduct of virtuous people and reason.[30] In another place, Manu even adds another source as 'that which is pleasing to oneself'.[31] The *Mahābhārata* refers to the Vedas, Smṛtis and conduct of the wise as sources of *dharma*.[32] In the *Śāntiparvan*, we are told, that, in case there is some doubt regarding *dharma*, ten or three scholars having a thorough knowledge of the Vedas should be asked to decide the matter.[33] In the *Mahābhārata*, *dharma* has been used in many senses. There are the *sādhāraṇadharmas* which echo the '*ṛta*' component of *dharma*, and then there are the *varṇāśramadharma*, *rājadharma*, *prajādharma*, *deśadharma*, *kuladharma*, *jātidharma*, etc. The *Mahābhārata*, as an epic concerned with the exploits of kings, devotes much of its attention to the *rājadharmas*, and goes to the extent of saying that *dharma* of the land depends entirely on the king.[34] It says further that the king is the maker of the four ages.[35]

A large section of the Śāntiparvan, which itself forms one-sixth of the *Mahābhārata* is devoted to the *dharma* in times of distress styled *āpaddharma*, or the *dharma* of abnormal times. All the violations of *dharma* are sought to be explained away and justified by resorting to *āpaddharma*. One can only say that 'each character in the *Mahābhārata* was aware of the framework of *dharma*, and when faced with a choice, chose according to his or her lights'.[36] This is brought out clearly in the behaviour of different characters in the *Mahābhārata*.

Let us take the case of Dhṛtarāṣṭra first. While *kuladharma* and *rājadharma* make it obligatory for him to treat the Pāṇḍavas and the Kauravas as his own sons and as equals, his dilemma is his natural inclination against the dictates of *dharma*. Before the Pāṇḍavas left for Khāṇḍavaprastha, Dhṛtarāṣṭra spoke to Yudhiṣṭhira with love and affection.[37] He warned him about his sons and bid him a fond farewell. But very soon Duryodhana, backed by Śakuni and Karṇa, persuaded him to invite Yudhiṣṭhira to a game of dice which was planned to deceive and destroy the Pāṇḍavas. Dhṛtarāṣṭra, thus, became a party to the shameful happenings at the Hastināpura court. When Vidura advised him against this, he could only blame destiny and the law of *karma*; and like a weak man said: 'If fortune favours us I have no fear regarding this game. If, on the contrary, fortune goes against us, how could we help it? For destiny is all powerful. Go and invite Yudhiṣṭhira on my behalf to come and play dice.'[38] There was nothing wrong in inviting Yudhiṣṭhira to a game of dice as it was a common pastime of kings in those times. But there were certain rules of the game, and one of them was that gambling was allowed but not betting.[39] Moreover, only inanimate objects could be staked as pawns and not living beings. All these rules were violated in this much-quoted game of dice at the court of Dhṛtarāṣṭra, and the only moral defence was that it was his fate.

Even after the Mahābhārata war was over and when the Pāṇḍavas went to greet him and pay their respects to the elders, Dhṛtarāṣṭra was unable to contain his anger and crushed the iron pillar thrust into his arms thinking it to be Bhīma. Dhṛtarāṣṭra's only defence against this consistent misbehaviour was that Duryodhana was the son born of his own body, while the Pāṇḍavas were not so. He further asks: 'How can you ask me to sacrifice my own body for those of others?'[40] In this context, it is interesting to note that Baudhāyana mentions an ancient writer Aupajanghani 'for the view that only an *aurasa putra* was to be recognised and not the other kinds of sons'.[41]

As against this we have the character of Bhīṣma whose personal life was a triumph of *dharma*. However, Bhīṣma's dilemma was being on the side of Duryodhana, and thus being a party to all the *adhārmic* actions of the Kauravas. In his personal life, Bhīṣma stuck to the path of *dharma* which brings us back to the *ṛta* component in latter day *dharma*. While the growth of institutions and the proliferation of different groups of people made it difficult to maintain uniformity in the various *dharmas* like the *varṇāśrama-dharma*, etc. it was still possible to stick to one's *dharma* in one's personal life. It is possibly with this idea that the *sādhāraṇa-dharmas* were incorporated into the *Dharmasūtras* and Smṛtis over and above the institutionalized *dharmas*.

The *sādhāraṇadharmas* are generally mentioned as *ahiṁsā*, *satya*, *asteya*, *brahmacarya* and *aparigraha*.[42] The *Mahābhārata* mentions the *sādhāraṇadharmas* at many places which sometimes agree with the above five and at times mentions many others as well. Amongst them truth has been given importance.[43] Others mentioned are control over the senses, forgiveness, regard for one's mother, father and the preceptor, good behaviour, agreeable speech, protecting a suppliant, hospitality towards a guest and so on.[44] The *Mahābhārata* has, thus, incorporated all that was recognized as *dharma* from time to time in its long history of growth. That the *sādharaṇadharmas* qualify as the *ṛta* component is also suggested by their inclusion in such philosophical texts as the *Yogasūtras* of Patañjali[45] and in the later *prakaraṇagranthas* of Vedānta.[46] In these philosophical texts, the task of *dharma* was to arouse the spiritual side in human beings and lead them to *mokṣa* (liberation). Even these texts divided the spiritual aspirant into an excellent, middling or inferior one, depending on the observance of various spiritual means, in which were included the *sādhāraṇadharmas*, also called the *yamas*. Only one who is an advanced *yogī* can practise these *yamas* unconditionally, and then it is called the *mahāvrata*.[47] The Jains also had a similar classification for the *śrāvaka* and the '*śramaṇa*' known respectively as *aṇuvrata* and *mahāvrata*.[48] What is implicit in all this classification is the difficulty faced by one engaged in fulfilling his *varṇa-śramadharma*, while observing the *sādhāraṇadharmas*.

But people like Bhīṣma and Vidura not only fulfilled their *varṇāśramadharmas* but they also worked out a compromise between these two conflicting rules of conduct. This they achieved by sticking to the *sādhāraṇadharmas* in their personal life, even while discharging their duties as true citizens of the land. Bhīṣma, who was devoted to *dharma*, did not approve of Duryodhana's *adhārmic* acts, but his *dharma* which dictated obedience to the king prevented him from deserting the Kauravas.

In his personal life, Bhīṣma never once told a lie, and he lost his life because he would not fight a woman as the *Dharmasūtras* prohibit the killing of a woman.[49] He stuck to the rules of warfare when he refused to fight Paraśurāma who was on foot, while he was seated on a chariot.[50] Having given his word to a life of unbroken chastity, he never once broke his promise. But when it came to obeying his king, Bhīṣma was a loyal citizen. The king and his *dharma* (*rājadharma*) have a sacred character in the *Mahābhārata*. Bhīṣma himself says that the king is appointed by Viṣṇu himself, and he partakes of his divinity and is, therefore, to be obeyed.[51] He is the protector of *dharma*, and it is due to fear of the king that people do not trouble others.[52] Manu also mentions that, in the absence of a king, stronger people eat weaker ones like the bigger fish devouring the smaller ones.[53] The king is even considered to be the maker of heaven on earth.[54] Thus, prosperity in the land and of his subjects depend on him.[55]

While thus speaking highly of the character and institution of kingship in general, the *Mahābhārata* makes a distinction between normal and abnormal times. While *dharma* can only be practised towards one who is *dhārmic*, the *Mahābhārata* sanctions *adhārmic* behaviour towards an *adhārmic* person. A whole chapter is devoted to *dharma* during abnormal times which is called *āpad-dharma*.[56] This, in short, sanctions any means in order to achieve the desired end.

The normal rules of *dharma* break down during *āpattikāla*. The *Mahābhārata* does not hesitate to say that protecting one's life is the paramount duty during *āpattikāla*. In order to accomplish that, the *Mahābhārata* even advocates giving up one's family, kingdom and wealth. All the *dharmas* can be given up during *āpattikāla*. Bhīṣma himself says in one place: 'For one, who, is in distress, escape even by an improper path is allowed'.[57] Thus, the conflict and dilemma that Bhīṣma or any of the upright characters in the *Mahābhārata* should have normally faced is not there, and it leaves one disappointed. One expects Bhīṣma to stand up and speak against the *adhārmic* acts of Duryodhana; in fact, one feels that if he had felt strongly about Duryodhana's acts, he would have spoken up. The characters in the *Mahābhārata* are used to saying what they feel like, and, therefore, one has to conclude that if Bhīṣma suffered any moral conflict he chose to suppress it.

One is reminded of Vibhīṣaṇa in the *Rāmāyaṇa* who deserted his brother Rāvaṇa as he could not reconcile himself to the conduct of his brother. But there is no such character in the *Mahābhārata*. Even Vidura, though well known for his partiality for the Pāṇḍavas, did not undergo any serious mental conflict which would have forced him to leave the Kaurava camp. Balarāma perhaps underwent a deep moral conflict which prompted him to stay away from the Kurukṣetra battle. Since he had equal affection for both the Pāṇḍavas and the Kauravas, he decided not to take sides in the battle. One has thus to conclude that, while problems giving rise to moral dilemma or moral conflict exist in ample measure in the *Mahābhārata*, they are all subsumed either under the law of *karma* and human destiny, or under the *dharma* that prevails in times of distress.

If we look at the woman characters in the *Mahābhārata*, the impression is created that they were there appendages to the main characters; and, though there were burst of protests at times, they were ignored, and the women were asked to conform to the position in society assigned to them. The most pathetic of the female characters is that of Gāndhārī. A princess by birth and a queen by marriage, she blindfolded herself on learning that her husband was blind. Did anybody even bother to champion her cause or dissuade her from this extreme action? There seems to be no protest even from her own brother Śakuni who stayed at the Kaurava court. She deprived herself of the coverted joy of a mother gazing at the face of her offspring. She willingly sacrificed this as Dhṛtarāṣṭra could not have this joy. But she must have gone through great mental anguish and conflict; and, being a silent spectator of all the misdeeds of her family and others, resigned herself to what was in store by saying: 'Where there is *dharma* there will be victory.'[58] After the death of Duryodhana she posed questions on the use of deceit by Bhīma in killing Duryodhana. She says: 'I do not complain. But then in Vāsudeva's presence Bhīma called Duryodhana to battle, and, knowing that Duryodhana was stronger and could not be defeated in single combat, Bhīma struck him below the navel and killed him. Vāsudeva was looking on. This was wrong and it is this that I find it impossible to forgive.' She fails to understand how the *dharma* laid down by those who know *dharma* can be given up during war time.[59] This is her mental conflict, and the conflict of every woman condemned not to act but watch silently the misdeeds of those near and dear to her.

Kuntī had to suffer the fate of having her own son Karṇa fight her other sons. She faced a great dilemma before she decided to go and talk to him about the truth before the battle of Kurukṣetra. She had to confess her shame before her son, whom she had abandoned the moment he was born, and listen to his refusal to come back to the side of his brothers. Karṇa's reply to Kuntī in the Udyogaparvan[60] is well known for its sense of justice and fairplay. This was one of the rare occasions when Karṇa strictly followed the code of *dharma*.

Before concluding it is but proper to look at Draupadī who plays a pivotal role in the *Mahābhārata*, almost as important as that of Helen in the Trojan war. Yudhiṣṭhira lost everything in the game of dice including himself. He was then goaded to stake Draupadī in the game whom he again lost. Draupadī's question as to whether Yudhiṣṭhira had the right to pawn her after losing himself in the game gets no answer from anyone.[61] Even Bhīṣma could only say that he was unable to answer the question due to the subtlety of *dharma*. But one wonders what would have happened, if she was set free in answer to her query. The Pāṇḍavas being already slaves of the Kauravas, she would have been an orphan or a widow, though her husbands were still living.[62]

While the *Mahābhārata* allows its women to shout and ran at the injustices and also allows them freedom to choose their husbands or live as they please,[63] the rules laid down by Manu and the other *Dharmasūtras* were well entrenched. *Pativratādharma* and the chastity of woman were praised as the highest *dharma* for women, and this is brought out clearly in the story of Kauśika and the crow in the *Virāṭaparvan*.[64]

Thus, the women of the *Mahābhārata* suffered from great mental torture, and their dilemma was and still is that of having to agree to whatever is decided by the men of their family, though it may be against their conviction. While the *sādhāraṇadharmas* were aimed at the men, for the women, serving their husbands was the only *dharma* prescribed and in that sense there was no differences from the stand that Manu took, i.e. 'a woman does not deserve independence'.[65]

Thus, the question of moral dilemmas or moral conflicts in the *Mahābhārata* is not easy to understand. One realizes the predicament of Dhṛtarāṣṭra, of Gāndhārī, of Kuntī, of Karṇa, of Yudhiṣṭhira, of Arjuna in the famous speech immortalized in the beginning of the *Bhagavadgītā*; of Bhīṣma, of Droṇa and many other characters. The dilemma is never brought to the forefront as a 'dilemma', but is subsumed under either as duties which fall under certain institutions like the *varṇāśramadharma* or justified because of certain actions and the power of human destiny.

NOTES

1. *Arthaśāstramidam proktam dharmaśāstramidam mahat*
   Kāmaśāstramidam proktam vyāsenāmitabuddhinā.
   Mahābhārata, Ādiparvan.
2. *Yadihāsti tadanyatra yannehāsti na tadkvacit.*
   Ibid., Svargārohaṇaparvan.
3. P.V. Kane, *History of Dharmaśāstra*, vol. i. pt. Pune, Bhandarkar Oriental Research Institute, 1968, pp. 358-73.
4. P.V. Kane, *Ibid.*, pp. 349.
5. Pratima Bowes, *The Concept of Morality*, London, George Allen & Unwin Ltd., 1959, pp. 166-69.
6. *The Mahābhārata*, Droṇaparvan.
7. *Ibid.*, Gadāparvan, tr. C. Rajagopalachari, *Mahābhārata*, p. 373.
8. *The Mahābhārata*, Svargārohaṇaparvan.
9. *Yato dharmastato jayaḥ.*
10. *Nityo dharmaḥ sukhaduḥkhe tvanitye.*
11. P.V. Kane, *Ibid.*, p.1.
12. *Ibid.*, pp. 3-4.
13. M. Hiriyanna, *Outlines of Indian Philosophy*, London, George Allen & Unwin Ltd., 1951, p. 33.

14. *Ibid.*, p. 34.
15. Manorama Jauhari, *Politics and Ethics in Ancient India*, Varanasi, Bharatiya Vidya Prakashan, 1968, p. 74.
16. *Ibid.*, p. 74.
17. *Athāto dharmam vyākhyāsyāmaḥ yatobhyudayaniḥśreyasasiddhiḥ sa dharmaḥ.*
18. *The Mahābhārata*, Śāntiparvan.
19. *Gobrāhmaṇanṛpastrīṣu sakhyurmāturgurostathā,*
Vṛddhabālajaḍāndheṣu na śastrāṇyupadhārayet.
20. *Ibid.*, Śāntiparvan.
21. T.S. Rukmani, *A Critical Study of the Bhāgavata Purāṇa*, Chowkhamba Sanskrit Series, vol. lxxvii, Varanasi, 1970, p. 92.
22. *itihāsapurāṇābhyām vedam samupabṛṁhayet,*
bibhetyalpaśrutādvedo māmayaṁ pratariṣyati.
23. P.V. Kane, *ibid.*, p. 50.
24. *Manusmṛti*, ix, 56-63.
25. *Ibid.*, ix, 64-68.
26. *Yājñavalkyasmṛti*, II, 131.
27. Kauṭilya, *Arthaśāstra*, iii, 6 and i. 17.
28. P.V. Kane, *ibid.*, p. 539.
29. The *Mahābhārata*, Striparvan.
30. *Manusmṛti*, ii, 6.
31. *Ibid.*, ii, 12.
32. *The Mahābhārata*, Vanaparvan, Anuśāsanaparvan, Śāntiparvan.
33. *Ibid.*, Śāntiparvan.
Daśa vā vedaśāstrajñastrayo vā dharmapāṭhakāḥ,
Yadbrūyuḥ kārya utpanne sa dharmo dharmasaṃśayo.
34. *Ibid.*,
Niyantā cenna vidyeta na kaścid dharmamācaret.
35. *Ibid.*, Udyogaparvan.
Rājā kṛtayugasraṣṭā tretāyā dvāparasya ca,
Yugasya ca caturthasya rājā bhavati kāraṇam.
36. Iravati Karve, *Yugānta: The End of an Epoch*, Sangam Books, Orient Longmans Ltd., 1974. p. 171.
37. *The Mahābhārata*, Ādiparvan.
38. *Ibid.*, Sabhāparvan.
39. *Manusmṛti*, ix, 223.
40. Iravati Karve, *ibid.*, p. 167.
41. P.V. Kane, *ibid.*, p. 539.
42. *Manusmṛti*, vi, 70.
43. *The Mahābhārata*, Ādiparvan.
44. These are found all over in the various *parvans* of the *Mahābhārata.*
45. *Patañjali Yogasūtra*, ii, 31.
46. Sadānanda, *Vedāntasāra*, pp. 111ff.
47. *Yogasūtra*, ii, 31.
48. M. Hiriyanna, *ibid.*, p. 167.

49. *Na strīyam hantumarhasi.—The Mahābhārata* Ādiparvan.
Strīṣu goṣu na śastrāṇi pātayed brāhmaṇeṣu ca—Ibid., Sabhāparvan.
50. *The Mahābhārata*, Udyogaparvan.
51. *Ibid.*, Śāntiparvan.
52. *Prajā rājabhayādeva na khādanti parasparam.—Ibid.*, Śāntiparvan.
53. *Manusmṛti*, viii, 20.
54. *Kāmandaka*, i. 9.
55. *The Mahābhārata*, Udyogaparvan.
56. (*a*) *Bhavatyadharmo dharmo hi dharmāharmāvubhāvapi,*
Kāraṇaddeśakālasya deśakālaḥ sa tādṛśaḥ.
Ibid., Śāntiparvan.
(*b*) *Anyo dharmaḥ samarthānāmāpatsvanyaśca bhārata,*
Tasmādāpatsvadharmopi śrūyate dharmalakṣaṇah.
Ibid., Śāntiparvan.
57. *Pīḍitasya kimudvāramutpatho vidhṛtasya ca,*
Advārataḥ pradravati yathā bhavati paṇḍitaḥ.
Ibid., Śāntiparvan.
58. *Ibid.*, Strīparvan.
59. *Ibid.*, Śāntiparvan.
60. *Ibid.*, Śāntiparvan.
61. *Ibid.*, Sabhāparvan.
62. Iravati Karve, *ibid.*, p. 88.
63. *The Mahābhārata*, Ādiparvan, 113ff.
64. *Ibid.*, Virāṭaparvan.
65. *Manusmṛti: na strī svātantryamarhati.*

THE CONCEPT OF MORAL DILEMMA: ITS APPLICABILITY IN THE CONTEXT OF THE MAHĀBHĀRATA

S.P. DUBEY

A DILEMMA involves a crisis of choice between two or more alternatives. It arises in a situation where it is difficult to choose either one or the other course of action. Usually it is a situation of 'neither-nor' when one is in a quandary, and can do neither this nor that. One then has to have recourse to passivity, which at times arouses a sense of guilt in one's mind. The sense of guilt usually arises in a moral situation where one is unable to act according to one's normative inclination.

Moral dilemma can be said to arise in a moral situation involving a confrontation of alternatives of a seemingly equivalent nature. The expression 'seemingly' is being used specifically in this context, because the term 'equivalent' is hard to determine in the normative realm. In the ethical context, it is difficult to find exactly equivalent situations. All we can say is that the alternatives may be more or less equivalent. This is mostly so, because moral judgement depends on objective considerations; but it requires subjective determination as well. In any concrete situation, the ideal of morally objective judgements is neither fully possible nor plausible.

In the *Mahābhārata* moral dilemmas (*dharmapāśa*) are faced by many characters on various occasions. The stories of the epic have moulded the life and thinking of our country for centuries and continue to do so in the present. They will also continue to shape the Indian ethos for ages to come. Sukthankar, after many years of intensive study of the epic, while preparing the critical edition, rightly said: 'We are it: I mean the real we.'[1]

The *Mahābhārata* teaches us that the real conquest is not achieved in the battlefield. There is a battle going on within man on his own lower nature, and it must be won. The epic has always emphasized the fact that the ultimate victory is that of righteousness (*dharma*). This is why the work is known as the *Jaya*, as is evident from the very first verse.[2] The fact that moral integrity ultimately prevails is realized and expressed by several important figures of the *Mahābhārata* on different occasions. The author of the epic, Kṛṣṇa Dvaipāyana Vyāsa, warns King Dhṛtarāṣṭra of the consequences of favouring the path of unrighteousness by his one hundred sons. He clearly tells the blind ruler that where there is *dharma* there will be victory.[3] Bhīṣma repeats this to Duryodhana (initially designated as Suyodhana) when the latter charges the old general with favouring the Pāṇḍavas on the battlefield.[4] Droṇa, the teacher of both groups in the art of using arms, tells Yudhiṣṭhira that where there is moral integrity there Kṛṣṇa is, and where Kṛṣṇa is there is victory.[5] Even Karṇa confesses in his secret talks with Kṛṣṇa that Yudhiṣṭhira is the lasting ruler since he is the embodiment of *dharma*.[6]

Although the *Mahābhārata* is taken to be a treatise on *dharma* (moral integrity), it is not a *dharmaśāstra* since it does not deal exclusively with morality. It also contains the art of creating and exploiting economic resources (*artha*) and the science of eroticism or aesthetic activity (*kāma*).[7] In fact, it is a treatise on the three goals of human life, popularly known as *trivarga*. The author of the epic, at the end of the massive composition. laments (virtually the entire society of his time), because people are unable to understand the maxim that prosperity and pleasure arise from moral integrity.[8]

The Indian tradition, as depicted in the *Mahābhārata*, does not treat the three goals of the individual (*puruṣārtha*) as independent of each other. Although the hierarchy of values is always admitted and maintained, the integral view of life has been preferred. The fourth or the ultimate goal of life, namely, *mokṣa* (salvation), is not much emphasized in the epic. It is implicit in the text that righteous living and moral integrity will automatically lead one to salvation. Explicit statements, of course, are not lacking, but *dharma* is definitely given importance as the immediate means to salvation. The remaining two goals are taken to be subservient to *dharma*, and are supposed to be regulated by it.

Since man is a moral agent, conflicts in his moral perception take place arising from a clash of the means and end. The author of the epic shows that those who subordinate virtue to wealth land themselves in trouble and are led to total destruction, as happens in the case of the Kauravas. In the Pāṇḍavas' camp, Yudhiṣṭhira stands for moral integrity and righteousness. The other four brothers believe in the interdependence of wealth and virtue. After the war is won they discuss the propriety of Yudhiṣṭhira's desire to become an ascetic. They virtually subscribe to Kauṭilya's theory that all is well provided one does not violate virtue or wealth. Draupadī also pursuades Yudhiṣṭhira to accept the kindgdom once it has been won.[9]

The major clash in the epic is, time and again, between moral integrity and the needs of survival and prosperity. The Pāṇḍavas are willing to forego the rights of the kingdom if five villages are given to them. On some occasions, they are even ready to give up this demand. Arjuna, when confronted with his elders, relatives, and teachers on the battlefield, refuses to take up arms against them even if they kill him.[10] Yudhiṣṭhira tells Kṛṣṇa that he will go to the forest, because he has no interest in the war in view of Bhīṣma's constant pressure on the Pāṇḍavas' army.[11]

The Kauravas, on their part, hardly give preference to moral integrity. They usually pursue prosperity and pleasure. Dhṛtarāṣṭra is normally convinced by them about the propriety of their stand to victimize the Pāṇḍavas. At times the blind king feels suffocated, but succumbs to the pressure of his sons. The only time Dhṛtarāṣṭra behaves gracefully is when he makes Draupadī (also known as Kṛṣṇa) and her husbands free after the first gambling between Yudhiṣṭhira and Śakunī (representing the Kauravas, being their maternal uncle).[12] That, too, happens when the *sāḍī* of Draupadī is extended by divine agency (Kṛṣṇa) and after ominous signs having been witnessed in the Yajñaśālā of the Kauravas.

There is a group of nobles in the Kauravas' camp who stand for moral integrity and righteousness, but are often silent mainly because of their financial obligations. Bhīṣma, Droṇācārya, and Kripācārya feel that the Pāṇḍavas are just; but they fail to favour them openly, because they are obliged to the Kauravas for their livelihood. Bhīṣma clearly tells Yudhiṣṭhira that man is the slave of wealth, whereas wealth is no one's slave; and that he himself is bound by the Kauravas' wealth.[13] He feels helpless on account of this obligation, and asks to be excused for his stand.[14] Droṇa and Kripa also, although willing to help Yudhiṣṭhira in his righteous cause, fail to extend their support only because of their financial obligation.[15]

We can find three figures in the *Mahābhārata* who do not appear to experience moral dilemmas. They are Duryodhana, Karṇa and Kṛṣṇa. Duryodhana does not feel any dilemma, because he is blinded by greed and hatred against the Pāṇḍavas. He can neither listen to Vidura nor negotiate with Kṛṣṇa in the cause of peace. His close associate Karṇa also does not feel any moral crisis. This is mainly because Karṇa has been provided an honourable position and a state to rule by Duryodhana. His chivalrous character and integrity are almost unsurpassed. When Kuntī, his mother, requests him to stay away from the battle against the Pāṇḍavas, he tells her that he is helpless to obey her as people will think him disloyal if he dissociates from Duryodhana.[16] He, however, promises not to kill the Pāṇḍavas except Arjuna.[17]

Karṇa, further, defends the action of Duryodhana to disgrace Draupadī in the assembly after Yudhiṣṭhira loses the game (dice). He tells Draupadī that, since her husband has lost in the gambling, he (Yudhiṣṭhira) is a slave according to the conditions of the game; and a slave, disciple or son and wife are always dependent.[18] Being the wife of a slave she does not have the right of an independent voice in the assembly, hence she should go to the inner apartments of the Kauravas' palace and act like a maidservant.[19] He also rebukes Vikarṇa, the brother of Duryodhana, who pleads for Draupadī in the court, and tells him that, since this woman has got five husbands, she is like a prostitute; and one should not mind if she is being dishonoured in the court.[20] Bhīmasena, at this point, rightly says that Karṇa is speaking as any slave should in tune with the *dāsadharma*. Karṇa does not mind these words. He, however, grudges the independence of Bhīṣma, Droṇa and Vidura in the assembly, who, according to social norms, should have been more loyal and felt indebted to the Kauravas since they were economically dependent on the Kauravas.

The strong chivalrous character of Karṇa makes him jealous of Bhīṣma as well as Arjuna. He clearly tells Duryodhana that he will not take part in the war as long as the command of the Kauravas' army remains in the hands of the old general. He is jealous of Arjuna because of Draupadī. He was not allowed to participate in the arrow-shooting arranged for the *svayaṁvara* (self-election selection of the husband by the bride) of Draupadī and in which Arjuna could succeed in getting the hand of the princess. He denounces Arjuna when the latter does not allow a break in fighting when the wheel of his chariot got stuck in the mud.[21] In brief, Karṇa maintains his loyalty to the Kauravas, and remains consistent in his behaviour.

Śrī Kṛṣṇa being God incarnate, also usually does not feel any moral crisis. He is clear about his stand and consistently supports the cause of the Pāṇḍavas. He argues with his brother Balarāma and justifies a war to re-establish the Pāṇḍavas.[22] In his discussions with Sañjaya, the envoy of King Dhṛtarāṣṭra, he states that as a last resort to recover higher values even war is not immoral. He stresses the need for subscribing to the maintenance of social order (*lokasaṁgraha*)[23] for the good of all. He reminds the ambassador of the ill-treatment given to Draupadī in the assembly by the Kauravas. He, of course, is for a compromise between the two sides, and tells Sañjaya that the Kauravas and Pāṇḍavas are like the forest and the tigers who should protect each other.[24] However, when all the efforts to reach an honourable settlement fail, he asks Yudhiṣṭhira to fight. He also persuades Arjuna as well when arch the warrior felt disgusted at the sight of his dear ones lined up to fight against one another. He goes to the extent of breaking his promise not to take to arms against the Kauravas in the battlefield when Bhīṣma was about to overpower the Pāṇḍavas.[25] He assures Yudhiṣṭhira that, if Arjuna does not kill Bhīṣma, he himself will kill the son of Gaṅgā.[26] But, in all circumstances, he keeps his promise, namely, to maintain the moral order in society in order to protect the values, virtues, and saintly qualities of man.[27]

The character of Devavrata, son of King Śāntanu from Gaṅga, when taken in its entire perspective, presents a unique example of moral integrity. Devavrata, one of the eight Vasus in his earlier life, becomes Bhisma because of his vow of lifelong celibacy to the boatman.[28] He also foregoes the right of succession to the throne, and promises the fisherman, the father of Satyavatī, that the child born of his stepmother Satyavatī shall be the heir of the kingdom of Hastināpura.[29] Satyavatī recognizes him as righteousness embodied in the family of the Kauravas.[30] He is supposed to be the manifestation of truth and the highest standard of morality. Lord Kṛṣṇa is also confident of his truthfulness. When the Pāṇḍavas are perplexed due to the furious assaults of Bhīṣma on the battlefield, Kṛṣṇa reminds Yudhiṣṭhira to go to the grandsire, and ask for the secret how he could be killed.[31] And Bhīṣma does tell Yudhiṣṭhira the secret of his death.

True to his vow, Bhīṣma does not allow any concession to celibacy. When Satyavatī herself requests him to help in the *niyoga* (intercourse with a woman to beget a child) with the widows of his stepbrother Vicitravīrya, he bluntly refuses to do so and says that he cannot break the vow since it was a precondition to her marriage with his father. In a long statement in the epic, he tells her that he would not give up truth even if the earth quits fragrance, fire its form, sun its heat, and moon its coolness, etc.[32] Even the kingdom of the three worlds is meaningless to him if compared to truth.[33] His determination is like that of Naciketas of the *Kaṭha Upaniṣad* when the child does not accept any other boon from Yama except the knowledge of the secrets of the self.

Bhīṣma never violates the accepted codes of the battle. He accepts the norms prescribed in the context, as stated by Kāpavya, that ladies, cowards, children, ascetics, and the reluctant ones in the fight should not be killed. He also knows that women should not be married forcibly.[34] He, further, knows that no one, except Kṛṣṇa and Arjuna, can kill him in the battlefield if he is ready with arms.[35] Therefore, he tells Yudhiṣṭhira that he can be killed by Arjuna if Śikhaṅdin (princess Ambā in her previous birth) is kept in front of Arjuna's chariot.[36] He tells Yudhiṣṭhira and Duryodhana alike that Śikhaṅdin was a woman in the previous birth, and he will not kill her even if he has to give up his life.[37] He also does not face Śrī Kṛṣṇa when the latter comes forward without arms (with the wheel of the chariot) to confront him in the battlefield. He, rather, welcomes the Lord, and wishes to be killed by Him for that would give him the highest position, namely, salvation.[38]

Bhīṣma confronts a moral dilemma when he forcibly captures the three daughters of the king of Kāśī in their *svayaṁvara* for his stepbrothers. He takes away all the three sisters, because he was ridiculed by the princes assembled in the court and also because he was laughed at by the princesses for his old age. When he brings the three sisters (Ambā, Ambikā and Aṁbālika) to the capital and arranges their marriage with Vicitravīrya, the eldest one, Ambā, refuses. Ambā insists on marrying Bhīṣma himself as it was he who abducted her from the court of her father. She makes an appeal to his honour, and asks him to act in accordance with the code of conduct in the context. Bhīṣma gets utterly confused for some time.[39] He tells her about his vow of celibacy, and requests her to marry his brother. Ambā, obviously, does not agree to do so. Bhīṣma then decides to send her to Śalva, the king of Saubha. It may be noted here that Śalva was already in love with Ambā. Ambā, on her part, also had developed a liking for Śalva with the consent of her father.[40] Hence Śalva had resisted Bhīṣma when the latter was taking the three sisters to Hastināpura. But he was humbled by Bhīṣma in the confrontation, and his life was spared by Bhīṣma at the instance of Ambā. But Śalva declines to marry Ambā as he still fears the wrath of Bhīṣma. He tells her to go back to Bhīṣma.[41] Back in Hastināpura, Ambā requests Bhīṣma again to oblige her but of no avail. Consequently, she curses Bhīṣma and approaches Paraśurāma, the teacher of Bhīṣma, for help.[42] Paraśurāma also failed to pursuade his disciple to marry Ambā. He fought a fierce duel with Bhīṣma but without any positive result. Due to utter frustration and extreme hatred, Ambā embraced death to be born again as Śikhaṇḍin in order to exact her revenge on him. She is born as the daughter of King Drupada, and subsequently changes her sex to become Śikhaṇḍin and one of the commanders of the Pāṇḍavas' forces.

Bhīṣma knows very well that the Pāṇḍavas are righteous. He blesses Yudhiṣṭhira and wishes him victory when the latter approaches the grandfather before the break of the war.[43] He tells Yudhiṣṭhira about his obligation towards Duryodhana because of his economic dependence.[44] But when Duryodhana charges him with being lenient towards the Pāṇḍavas on the battlefield, he clearly tells him that the Pāṇḍavas are invincible. And yet he promises to do his best in spite of old age.[45] He announces that next day he will not spare anyone on the battlefield except Śikhaṇḍin.[46] The Pāṇḍavas felt perplexed because of his furious assaults next day, and decided to place Śikhaṇḍin in front of Arjuna's chariot. This was the tenth day of the war. Now Arjuna started shooting arrows on Bhīṣma keeping Śikhaṇḍin in front. The old general, true to his words, kept his arms aside as he had decided not to kill a woman. He had learnt from the moral codes that women are not to be killed. When his body is pierced by arrows, he tries to take them out one by one and identifies most of them as those of Arjuna and not of Śikhaṇḍin.[47] Overwhelmed by grief he repeats this ten times. The great warrior is helpless. He cannot defend himself against the assaults from Arjuna, because he cannot make Arjuna his target since Śikhaṇḍin was placed in front of Arjuna's chariot. He bears the attacks without retaliation.

The helplessness of Bhīṣma is more acute in an earlier situation when Draupadī is being disgraced in the assembly of Dhṛtarāṣṭra. He, along with Droṇa, Kṛpa and few others, known for their wisdom and sense of judgement, is unable to restrain Duryodhana from sending Pratikāmin, followed by Duḥśāsana, to bring Draupadī in the assembly. Draupadī wanted to know whether Yudhiṣṭhira first lost her or himself.[48] She, of course, realizes on her part, that joy and suffering afflict everyone, and, in suffering especially, moral integrity (*dharma*) is of utmost value.[49] She tells the assembly that she will do whatever she is asked to, if she is told, after due considerations, whether she has been won or not.[50] Karṇa, Śakunī and the Kauravas (except Vikarṇa), obviously, were not touched by her appeal. But Vikarṇa is astonished why elders like Bhīṣma and Dhṛtarāṣṭra are keeping quiet, and why a great adviser like Vidura is holding his tongue.[51] Karṇa, as expected, retorts and asks him to be silent when seniors are present in the court. He also tries to establish the propriety of Duryodhana's decision, as we have seen above.

Bhīmasena, meanwhile, gets perturbed over the affair and tries to retaliate. But he soon realizes, like the other Pāṇḍavas, that he is bound by a specific code of conduct in the context (*dharmapāśa*).[52] He feels helpless and resorts to silence.

But the *dharmapāśa* is extremely perturbing for Bhīṣma, as he is supposed to be the custodian of righteousness in the Kauravas' court. He tells Draupadī that a wife must obey her husband but that a husband does not have the right to stake his wife.[53] He confesses that due to the subtle nature of *dharma* and the importance of the issues involved in her question he is unable to give a proper reply to her.[54] He also tells her that Yudhiṣṭhira can give up the entire world but not the truth, and, since he has already admitted that he has been defeated, the question cannot be answered properly.[55] It is important to note at this juncture that Vidura clearly states that Draupadī was not conquered, because Yudhiṣṭhira having lost himself to Śakunī had no right to bet her.[56] But Bhīṣma is not so clear about the matter, and tells Draupadī that Śakunī is unsurpassed in gambling and Yudhiṣṭhira has been won by him in the game. Since Yudhiṣṭhira does not treat his defeat as an act of cheating, he (Bhīṣma) is unable to answer the question adequately.[57]

Bhīṣma ultimately resorts to the subtle nature of *dharma*. He tells Draupadī that the course of morality is very subtle. Even the illustrious and wise in the world are unable to understand it.[58] He states that in this world what a strong man calls morality is regarded as such by others, whatever it may really be.[59] But about one point he is very sure. He tells Draupadī that the destruction of the Kauravas' race is imminent, because the Kauravas have become the slaves of coveteousness and folly,[60] and coveteousness is the source of sin.[61] He, further, praises the strong moral integrity of Draupadī,[62] and also points out that elders like Droṇa and others, even though conversant with moral codes, sit with their heads down because of their moral dilemma.[63]

Realizing his own complex position and his inability to answer the question of the noble lady, in all earnestness Bhīṣma refers her to Yudhiṣṭhira whom he treats as the authority on the question.[64] Yudhiṣṭhira could not speak at this moment. Arjuna, however, admits that Yudhiṣṭhira had full authority to put his brothers and wife at stake before he lost himself. But the fact was that he had lost himself first.

An ugly finale in the assembly, as noted earlier, is averted due to the miraculous extension of Draupadī's *sāḍī* and the ominous cries of dogs and jackals near the *yajñaśālā* which induced Dhṛtarāṣṭra to let her and the Pāṇḍavas be free[65] only to be trapped again by Duryodhana and Śakunī through the dice resulting in their thirteen years' exile before the great war broke out.

The moral dilemma of Bhīṣma is over when he decides not to fight against Śikhaṇḍin; and thus, although indirectly, he allows Arjuna to attack without offering any resistance. He opts for his death during *uttarāyaṇa* (when the sun moves northward from the tropic of Capricorn), since he is gifted with the power to control his death and to leave the physical body as and when he desires.[66] He lies down on a bed of arrows for fifty-eight days. At the instance of Lord Kṛṣṇa, he teaches Yudhiṣṭhira and all the others present there the code of conduct in different walks of life including moral crisis (see Śānti and Anuśāsana parvans of the epic). The long discourse covers almost the entire realm of individual and social life. It is unique in the history of human thought.

Since Dhṛtarāṣṭra was also present when Bhiṣma was preaching while preparing for his death, Bhīṣma requests him to look after the Pāṇḍavas as his own sons since they tread the path of righteousness.[67] The noble old man left this world in absolute peace and harmony. In the Indian tradition the name of Bhīṣma is recorded as synonymous with truthfulness and moral integrity.

REFERENCES

The verses quoted from the *Mahābhārata* in this paper are from the text edited by Satavalekar, unless otherwise specified.

1. V.S. Sukthankar, *Critical Studies in the Mahābhārata*, Pune, 1944, p. 439.
2. *Nārāyaṇaṁ namaskṛtya naraṁ caiva narottamam, devīṁ sarasvatīṁ caiva tato jayamudīrayet.* Invocation.
3. *Yato dharmastato jayaḥ. Mahābhārata*, Bhīṣmaparvan, 2.14.
4. *Ibid.*, 77.8; 85.43.
5. *Yato dharmastataḥ Kṛṣṇo yataḥ Kṛṣṇastato Jayaḥ. Ibid.*, 41.55.
6. *Sa eva rājā dharmātmā śāśvato'stu Yudhiṣṭhiraḥ.* Udyogaparvan, 139.23.
7. *Arthaśāstramidaṁ proktaṁ dharmaśāstramidaṁ mahat,*
   kāmaśāstramidaṁ proktaṁ Vyāsenā'mita-buddhinā
   Cf. Satvalakar, 'Introduction' in the *Mahābhārata*, p. 7.
8. *ūrdhvabāhurviromyeṣa na ca kaścicchṛṇoti me,*
   Dharmādarthaśca kāmaśca sa kimartaṁ na sevyate.
   Svargārohaṇaparvan, p. 49.
9. *Nādaṇḍaḥ Kṣatriyo bhāti nādaṇḍo bhūtimaśnute,*
   Nādaṇḍasya prajā rājñah sukhamedhanti Bhārata.
   Sabhāparvan, 14.14.

10. *The Bhagavadgītā*, 1.28-46.
11. *Vanaṁ yāsyāmi durdharṣa śreyo me tatra vaigatam,*
Na yuddhaṁ rocate Kṛṣṇa hanti Bhīṣma hi naḥ sadā,
Bhiṣmaparvan, 103.19.
12. Sabhāparvan, 63.27-36.
13. *Arthasya puruṣo dāso dāsastvartho na kasyacit,*
Iti satyam Mahārāja baddho' smyarthena Kauravaiḥ.
Bhīṣmaparvan, 41.36.
14. *Atastvaṁ klībavad vākyaṁ bravīmi Kurunandana,*
Bhṛtyo'smyarthena Kauravya yuddhādanyatkimicchasi.
Ibid., 41.37.
15. *Ibid.*, 41.51, 52 and 66.
16. *Na hi śakṣyāmahaṁ tyaktuṁ nṛpaṁ Duryodhanaṁ raṇe,*
anāryaṁ ca nṛśansaṁ ca kṛtaghnaṁ ca hi me bhavet.
Śāntiparvan, 1.28.
17. *Vadhyānviṣahyāṅsaṅgrāme na haniṣyāmi te sutān,*
Yudhiṣṭhiraṁ ca Bhīmaṁ ca yamau caivārjunādṛte.
Udyogaparvan, 144.20.
18. *Trayaḥ kileme adhanā bhavanti dāsaḥ śiṣyaścāsvatantrā ca nārī,*
Dāsasya patnī tvaṁ dhanamasya bhadre hīneśvarā dāsadhanaṁ ca dāsī.
Sabhāparvan, 61.1.
19. *praviṣya sā naḥ paricārairbhajasva tatte kāryaṁ śiṣtamāveśma veśma,*
Iśāh sma sarve tava rājaputri bhavantu te Dhārtarāṣṭra na Pārthāḥ
Ibid., 61.2
20. *Ibid.*, 61.36.
21. Karṇaparvan, 66·62.
22. Udyogaparvan, 1.10-24.
23. *Ibid.*, 29.1-51.
24. *Vanaṁ rājā Dhṛtarāṣṭraḥ saputro vyāghrā vane sañjaya pāṇḍaveyāḥ*
Mā vanaṁ chindi savyāghraṁ mā vyāghrānnīnaśo vanāt.
Udyogaparvan, 29.47.
Nirvano badhyate vyāghro nirvyāghraṁ chindyate vanaṁ,
Tasmādvyāghro vanaṁ rakṣedvanaṁ vyāghraṁ ca pālayet.
Ibid., 29.48.
25. Bhīṣmaparvan, 55.86-92; 102.37-58.
26. *Ibid.*, 55.82-85; 103.29-35.
27. *Paritrāṇāya sādhūnāṁ vināśāya ca duṣkṛtāṁ,*
Dharmasaṅsthāpanārthāya saṁbhavāmi yuge yuge.
Gītā, 4.8.
28. *Adya prabhṛti me dāsa brahmacaryaṁ bhaviṣyati*. Ādiparvan, 94.88.
29. *Yo'syāṁ janayiṣyate putra sa no rājā bhaviṣyati*. *Ibid.*, 94.79.
30. *Tvameva naḥ kule dharmastvaṁ satyaṁ tvaṁ parā gatiḥ*. *Ibid.*, 99.5.
31. *Gamyatāṁ sa vadhopāyaṁ pṛṣṭuṁ sāgaragā sutaḥ,*
Vaktumarhati satyaṁ sa tvayā pṛṣṭo viśeṣataḥ.
Bhīṣmaparvan, 103.51.
32. Ādiparvan, 97.1-18.

33. *Parityajeyaṁ trailokyaṁ rājyaṁ deveṣu vā punaḥ,*
Yadvāpyadhikatametābhyāṁ na tu satyaṁ kathañcana.
Ādiparvan, 97.15.
34. *Mā vadhīstvaṁ striyaṁ bhīrūṁ mā śiśuṁ mā tapasvīnāṁ*
Nā'yudhyamāno hantavyo na ca grāhyā balāt striyaḥ.
Śāntiparvan, 133.13.
35. *Na taṁ paśyāmi lokeṣu yo māṁ hanyātsamudyataṁ,*
Ṛte Kṛṣṇānmahābhāgāt Pāṇḍavādvā Dhanañjayāt.
Bhīṣmaparvan, 103.80.
36. *Ibid.*, 103.77.
37. *Ibid.*, 94.16-17; 108.18.
38. *Ibid.*, 102.60-61.
39. *Cintāmabhyagamadvīro yuktaṁ tasyaiva karmaṇaḥ.* Ādiparvan, 96.50.
40. *Mayā Saubhapatiḥ pūrvaṁ manasābhivṛtaḥ patiḥ,*
tena cāsmi vṛtā pūrvameṣa kāmaśca me pituḥ.
Ibid., 96.48.
41. *Gaccha gaccheti tāṁ Śālvaḥ punaḥ punarabhāṣata,*
Bibhemi Bhīṣmātsuśroṇi tvaṁ ca Bhīṣmaparigrahaḥ.
Udyogaparvan, 172.22.
42. *Ibid.*, 41.36.
43. *Prītosmi putrayuddhasva jayamāpnuhi Pāṇdava.* Bhīṣmaparvan, 41.34.
44. *Ibid.*, 41.36.
45. *Yattu śakyam mayā kartuṁ vṛddhenādya nṛpottama,*
Kariṣyāmi yathāśaktiṁ prekṣedānīm sabāndhavaḥ.
Ibid., 54.41.
46. *Ibid.*, 108.18.
47. *Arjunasya ime bāṇāḥ ne me bāṇāḥ Śikhaṇḍinaḥ,*
Nama prāṇānārūjanti ne me bāṇāḥ Śikhaṇḍinaḥ.
Ibid., 114.55-60.
48. *Kiṁ nu pūrvaṁ parājaiṣīrātmānaṁ māṁ nu Bhārata,* Sabhāparvan, 60.7.
49. *Evaṁ nūnaṁ vyadadhātsaṅvidhātā sparśāvubhau spṛśato dhīrabālau,*
dharmaṁ tvekaṁ paramaṁ prāha loke sa naḥ śamaṁ dhāṣyati gopyamānaḥ.
Ibid., 70.13.
50. *Saṁbhūya sarveśca jito'pi yasmātpaścādayaṁ kaitavamabhyupetaḥ,*
samikṣya sarve mama cā'pi vākyaṁ vibrūta me praśnamidaṁyathāvat.
Ibid., 61.44.
Jitaṁ vāpyajitaṁ vā'pi manyadhvaṁ vā yathā nṛpāḥ,
Tathā prayuktamicchāmi tatkariṣyāmi Kauravāḥ.
Ibid., 62.13.
51. *Bhīṣmaśca Dhṛtarāṣṭraśca Kuruvṛddhatamāvubhau,*
Sametya nāhatuḥ kiṇcidviduraśca mahāmatiḥ.
Ibid., 61.13.
52. *Dharmapāśasitastveyaṁ nādhigacchāmi saṅkaṭaṁ,*
Gauraveṇa niruddhaśca nigrahādarjunasya ca.
Ibid., 62.36.

53. *aśvo hyaśaktaḥ paṇituṁ parasvaṁ,*
striyaśca bharturvaśatāṁ samīkṣya. Ibid., 60.40.

54. *na vivektuṁ ca te praśnametaṁ śaknomi niścayāt,*
sūkṣmatvādgahanatvācca kāryasyāsya ca gauravāt. Ibid., 62.16.

55. *tyajeta sarvāṁpṛthivīṁ samṛddhāṁ yudhiṣṭhirah*
satyamatho na jahyāt/uktaṁ jito'smīti ca pāṇḍavena/
tasmānna śaknomi vivaktumetat. Ibid., 60.41.

56. *Ibid.*, 59.4.
57. *Ibid.*, 60.42.
58. *Uktavānasmi kalyāṇi dharmasya ca parāṁ gatiṁ,*
Loke na śakyate gantumapi viprairmahātmabhiḥ. Ibid., 62.14.

59. *Balavānstu tathā dharmaṁ loke paśyati pūruṣaḥ,*
Sa dharmo dharma-velāyāṁ bhavatyabhihitaḥ paraiḥ. Ibid., 62.15.

60. *Nūnamantaḥ kulasyāsya bhavitā na cirādiva,*
Tathā hi Kauravāḥ sarve lobhamohaparāyaṇāḥ. Ibid., 62.17.

61. *Eko lobho mahāgrāho lobhātpāpaṁ pravarttate.* Śāntiparvan, 152.2.
62. *Kuleṣu jātā Kalyāṇi vyasanābhyagatā bhṛśaṁ,*
Dharmānmārgānna cyavante yathā nastvaṁ vadhūḥ sthitā. Sabhāparvan, 62.18.

63. *Ete Droṇādayaścaive vṛddhā dharmavido janāḥ,*
Śūnyaiḥ śarīraistiṣṭhanti gatāsava ivānatāḥ. Ibid., 62.20.

64. *Yudhiṣṭhirastu praśne'sminpramāṇamiti me matiḥ,*
Ajitāṁ vā jitāṁ vāpi svayaṁ vyāhārtumarhati. Ibid., 62.21.

65. *Ibid.*, 63.27-36.
66. *Svacchaṅdamaraṇaṁ tasmai dadau tuṣṭaḥ pitā svayaṁ.* Ādiparvan, 94.94.

67. Anuśāsanaparvan, 153.33-34.

SELECT BIBLIOGRAPHY

ANCHAL, RAMESHWAR SHUKLA, *Aparājitā* (a poem on Aṁbā/Śikhaṇḍn), Meerut, 1983, p. 98.

CHAITANYA, KRISHNA, *The Mahābhārata: A Literary Study*, New Delhi, Clarion Books, 1985, pp. 462.

The Mahābhārata, ed. S.D. Satavalekar, 15 vols., Pārādī (dist. Balsad), Svadhyaya Mandala, 1968.

———, (cr. ed.), ed. Sukthankar and Karmarkar, 19 vols., Pune, Bhandarkar Oriental Research Institute, 1944-60.

———, (vol. 1), tr. & ed. J.A.B. Van Buitenen, University of Chicago Press, 1973.

MISHRA, D.P., *Krishnāyana* (rev.), ed. V.M. Sharma, Jabalpur, Lokmangal Prakashan, 1984, pp. 1280.

RAJAGOPALACHARI, C., *The Mahābhārata*, Bombay, Bharatiya Vidya Bhavan.

SUBRAMANIAM, KAMALA, *Mahābhārata*, Bombay, Bharatiya Vidya Bhavan, 1965, p. 766.

SUKTHANKAR, V.S., *On the Meaning of the Mahābhārata*, Bombay, Asiatic Society of Bombay, 1957 p. 146,

———, *Critical Studies in the Mahābhārata*, Pune, Memorial Committee, 1944, p. 440.

VAIDYA, C.V., *Mahābhārata* (abr.), Bombay, 1902.

VAIDYA, P.L., *Pratīka Index* (of *The Mahābhārata*), Pune, 1967.

A NOTE ON MORAL DILEMMAS IN THE MAHĀBHĀRATA

K. KUNJUNNI RAJA

IN GREAT literature as well as in real life, the problems that confront people in different situations are not based on the conflict between right and wrong, between *dharma* and *adharma*, but on the conflict between different and often opposing duties; between one's duty to one's kith and kin and that to society, between truth and non-violence, between what is immediately feasible and proper and what is ultimately correct. When there are opposing pulls from strong moral values, such as truth and non-violence, the problem is to determine the relative strength of these, and to decide what to do in the context. Is it enough if truth and non-injury are carried out literally or are the motive and intentions also to be taken into account? The *Mahābhārata*, unusually regarded as an encyclopaedia of Indian culture, dealing exhaustively with the aims of existence—*dharma*, *artha*, *kāma*, and *mokṣa*—is no exception to this general rule; and we find instances of moral dilemmas confronting the characters in many a situation. Before discussing a few instances from the *Mahābhārata*, the basic questions as to what is *dharma*, and whether it is absolute or flexible, and how to decide one's *dharma* have to be examined.

It is said in the *Mahābhārata* itself that the secret of *dharma* is hidden, and the only safe guide is to follow the practice of the people:

dharmasya tattvam nihitam guhāyām
mahājano yena gataḥ sa panthāḥ

Here the term *mahājano* has been interpreted in two ways: the majority of people, and good and wise men. Non-violence and truth are accepted as the two main features of the ethical code in every religion. But in the Dharmavyādha episode it is pointed out that absolute *ahiṁsā* is impossible, since we cannot avoid killing germs in water and in the air, and as far as the soul is concerned, it is immortal and no amount of *hiṁsā* can affect it. Also. the Smṛtis approve killing of violent attackers.

In the *Mahābhāratā* war, Bhīma killed his adversary Duryodhana by hitting him on the thigh which is against the rules of battle. When Gāndhārī reproached Bhīma for this, he defended himself on two grounds:

(*a*) The necessity of self-protection against a superior enemy; and
(*b*) As a revenge against Duryodhana for inviting Draupadī to sit on his lap, showing his bare thigh.

The well-known statement of Mārkaṇḍeya to Yudhiṣṭhira, *nese balasyeti cared adharmam*, interpreted in different ways, shows the flexible nature of *dharma*:

(1) One should not resort to *adharma*, thinking that one is strong;
(2) Non-violence by the weak is not real *dharma*; and
(3) If one refrains from violence, though one is strong, his act can be considered as *dharma*.

Bhīṣma's statement in the hall of gambling that 'whatever the strong man considers as *dharma* is taken to be *dharma*' is also significant. Of course, strength is not merely physical strength; intellectual strength is even more powerful than physical strength.

The most famous instance of moral dilemma in the *Mahābhārata* is that of Arjuna on the great battlefield when he found himself face to face with his elders and teachers. He is troubled, and his conscience revolts at the thought of the war and the mass murder it involves. Arjuna becomes the symbol of the tortured spirit of man which from age to age has been torn by conflicting obligations and moralities. The dilemma between individual duty and social responsibility is explained to him step by step by Kṛṣṇa to quell his agitation and remove his doubts. The *Bhagavadgītā* emphasizes devotion to duty without attachment or desire of reward as the ideal way of life for all people at all times.

One of the characters in the *Mahābhārata* who seems to be above all moral dilemmas is Kṛṣṇa himself, Kṛṣṇa who is the central figure in the story, who manipulates the working of fate through proper suggestions and hints, who is never afraid of *adharma*, knowing fully well that success in life cannot be achieved without resorting to what is normally considered as *adharma*. He even advises Yudhiṣṭhira to tell a white lie, *aśvathāmā hataḥ*, to make Droṇa believe that his son Aśvathāmā is dead.

One character who is always in a moral dilemma is Dhṛtarāṣṭra who means well but yields to the suggestion of Duryodhana, caught in a dilemma between affections towards his sons and what he feels as the proper thing to do. He explains his position aptly thus:

jānāmi dharmam na hi me pravṛttiḥ
jānāmyadharmam na hi me nivṛttiḥ
kenāpi devena hṛdisthitena
yathāniyuktosmi tathākaromi

One important problem about *dharma* is raised when Draupadī was staked by Yudhiṣṭhira in the game of dice after he had staked himself and lost. Vidura and Draupadī contended that Yudhiṣṭhira had lost all right to stake her, having first lost his own independence, since a slave had no right over his old possessions. Bhīṣma could not answer her properly, and remarked that the path of *dharma* is inscrutable, *dharmasya gahanā gatiḥ*. Even Vikarṇa supported Draupadī's stand. Bhīma was angry with Yudhiṣṭhira for having staked Draupadī, and Arjuna pacified him saying that his action was in the true spirit of a Kṣattriya. Here the point is that, though Yudhiṣṭhira has no legal right to stake Draupadī after staking himself and losing, Draupadī has a duty to see that his words were kept, for otherwise Dharmaputra will be a liar. Another point is that might was on the side of the Kauravas and whatever they did was right at that time. Bhīṣma puts it clearly:

balavānstu yathā dharmam loke paśyati pūruṣaḥ
sa dharmo dharmavelāyām bhavatyabhihitaḥ paraiḥ

His statement on Yudhiṣṭhira's truthfulness is also significant:

tyajeta sarvām pṛthivīm samṛddhām
Yudhiṣṭhiraḥ satyam atho na jahyāt

Later Yudhiṣṭhira himself regrets about the passive attitude taken by them at that time:

bhuyo'pi duhkham mama bhīmasena,
dūye visasyeva rasam viditvā
yad yājnasenīm parikṛṣyamānām
saṁdṛśya tat kṣāntamiti sma bhīma?

Yudhiṣṭhira was silent throughout, for he had no answer to solve the problem; even the elders like Bhīṣma and Droṇa did not give any decisive answer. The situation was saved only by Dhṛtarāṣṭra, who relented and consoled Draupadī and allowed the Pāṇḍavas to take back everything and return to Indraprastha.

Later, Yudhiṣṭhira was invited for a game of dice by Duryodhana for a second time. 'A challenge to dice cannot be refused by a Kṣattriya.' So again he played with Śakunī and again he lost; this time the stake was that the Pāṇḍavas would live in exile in the forest for twelve years and then one year incognito.

THE MEANING OF THE PURUṢĀRTHAS IN THE MAHĀBHĀRATA

Y. KRISHAN

THE word *puruṣārtha* signifies both human effort (*purusakāra*) as well as any object of pursuit (*artha*) of human beings. More specifically, it means anyone of the four aims or goals (*artha*) of man, viz. *dharma, artha, kāma, mokṣa.*

There is some controversy whether there were originally three (*trivarga*)[1] or four (*caturvarga*) *puruṣārthas*, the *trivarga* consisting of *dharma, artha* and *kāma*, the fourth *puruṣārtha mokṣa* being a latter addition. In fact, the Cārvākas considered *kāma* as the only goal of life (*kāma evaikaḥ puruṣārthah*), the *artha* being merely the means or instrument for realizing *kāma*. From this standpoint, in the *trivarga* classification both *dharma* and *artha* are merely the means and *kāma* the end, whereas in the *caturvarga* classification it is *mokṣa* which becomes the end, the ultimate goal; the other three *puruṣarthas* being the means to achieve *mokṣa*. To overcome this difficulty, sometimes the last *puruṣārtha* is called the *parama-puruṣārtha*.

Manusmṛti (2.224) explains the importance of all the three *puruṣarthas*. Some say *dharma* and *artha* are the best; others *kāma* and *artha*, and others *dharma* only; yet others *artha* only. But the real truth is that *sreya*, i.e. prosperity or welfare consists in and is achievable by all three together.

WHAT IS *dharma*?

The word *dharma* is a complex term having many meanings. Commonly it stands for religious beliefs and practices. It also refers to the codes of duties of social, political, economic institutions and entities. Medhatithi and Govindarāja, in their commentaries on Manu, explain *dharma* as fivefold: *varṇa-dharma*, caste duties; *āsramadharma*, duties of persons in the different stages of social life; *varnāsramadharma, naimittaka dharma*, occasional or periodical rites and ceremonies including *prāyaścitta*; expiratory rites and *guṇa dharma*, specific duties (of an institution or authority such as the duties of a king also called *rājadharma*).[2] Examples of other *dharmas* are: *kuladharma*, duties of a family; *strīdharma*, the duties of a woman; *jātīdharma*, caste duties; *śreṇidharma*, duties of corporations, etc. The meaning of the word *dharma* depends upon the context in which it is used, that is, the meaning is contextual or situational. Thus *Manusmṛti* (1.108) manitains: *acārāh paramo dharmaḥ*: good conduct is the excellent *dharma*. *Manusmṛti* (2.12) says:

> *vedaḥ smṛtiḥ, sadācāraḥ*
> *svasya ca priyam ātmanaḥ/*
> *etaccaturvidham prāhuḥ*
> *sākṣād dharmasya lakṣaṇam//*

The Veda, the sacred tradition, the custom followed by virtuous persons, and one's own pleasure, are the visible fourfold characteristics of *dharma*.

Again, Manu and Yājñavalkya identified *dharma* with *daṇḍa*, state power.

Yaj 1.35 says *dharmo hi daṇḍa rūpeṇa brahmaṇā mirmitaḥ*, the Brahman fashioned *dharma* in the shape of *daṇḍa*. *Manusmṛti* 7.18 reiterates: *daṇḍaṁ dharmaṁ*. The Vaiśeṣika's[3] call as *dharma* that which is responsible for prosperity (*abhyudaya*) as well as for final emancipation (*niḥśreyas*). The Mīmāṁ sakas[4] gave a utilitarian definition of *dharma*: *vedena prayojanam uddiśya vidhīyamāno artho dharmaḥ*. To Yājñavalkya and other law givers *dharma* comprehends *ācāra*, *vyavahāra* and *prāyaścitta*. *Ācāra* deals with religious practices including ethics or moral principles and *prāyaścitta* with religious rites including voluntary physical suffering for wrong doing. In short, the word *dharma* has to be interpreted contexually. In the context of the *puruṣārthas*, *dharma* essentially means *vyavahāra*, usage, ordinance, which define a man's duties in society, justice (*nyaya*). Medhatithi[5] on *Manusmṛti* 2.1 calls it *kartavyatā* (duty). *Mītāksarā* speaks of *sādhāranadharma*, duties common to all citizens. The *Mahābhārata* 3.149.28, in the context of the *puruṣārthas*, also defines *dharma* somewhat similarly: *ācāra sambhayo dharmo dharmād-vedāḥ samutthitāḥ*: *dharma* has its origin in good practices, and the Vedas are established in the *dharma.*

Importance of dharma

Of all the *puruṣārthas*, *dharma* is considered to be of the greatest importance. The *Mahābhārata* 5.122.35 states that those who desire *kāma* and *artha* should practise *dharma*, because *artha* and *kāma* cannot be separated (*apetya*). Further, *dharma* is the sole means of attaining *trivarga.*[6] The *Mahābhārata* 5.122.32 avers that it is through *dharma* that *artha* and *kāma*, in fact any objective, is fulfilled: *dharmādarthasca kāmasca sa kim artho na sevyate.* So it asserts that all enterprises should be consistent with *trivarga*, i.e. *dharma*, *artha* and *kāma*. But in case this becomes impossible, then these must be consistent with *dharma* and *artha*. In the *Mahābhārata* 7.126.35 it is said that *dharma* plays the principal (*pradhāna*) role in relation to *artha* and *kāma* while it is mentioned (the *Mahābhārata* 9.59.18) that a person attains happiness when there is no clash between *dharma* and *artha*, *dharma* and *kāma*, and *kāma* and *artha; dharmārthau dharmakāmau ca kāmārthau cāpyapīdayan.*[7] *Dharma* provides direction to *artha* and *kāma*. It provides the self-discipline essential for the beneficial pursuit of other two *puruṣārthas*. That is why *Cāṇakyasutra* declares: *sukhasya mūlam dharmāḥ; dharma* is the root of happiness.

It is thus *dharma* that leads to the behaviour which promotes harmony in society, facilitates its growth, and ensures its happiness: *na tatpareṣu kurvīta jānannapriyamātmanah*: one should not do unto others which is unpleasant to oneself (the *Mahābhārata* 12.251.19). Again, *yadyadātmani iccheta tatparasyāpi cintayeta*: whatever one desires for oneself one should desire the same for others (the *Mahābhārata* 12.251.21). These maxims declare offences against persons and property to be violations of *dharma*.

WHAT IS *artha*?

Like the word *dharma*, the word *artha* also has many meanings:[8]

(*i*) aim, purpose, cause, motive, reason, advantage, utility, use; (*ii*) thing, object, substance, wealth, property, opulence, money.

In the context of the *puruṣārthas*, *artha* means the aim of acquiring wealth, property, economic means of subsistence, viz. food, shelter, clothing and material life in general.

Importance of artha

According to the *Mahābhārata* 12.8.86, *artha* is the basis of prosperity, of development: *arthebhyo hi vivṛddhebhyaḥ*. *Cāṇakya-sūtra* 2 says: *dharmasya mūlam artha*: *artha* is the root of *dharma*; and in *Sutra* 92 it is stated: *arthasya mūlam kāryam;* work is the source of *artha*.

Sources of artha

One of the sources of *artha*, according to *Mahābhārata* 112.58.12, is effort, exertion (*utthāna*). *Utthāna* is the root of *rājadharma*; *utthānam hi narendrānām rājadharmasya mūlam* (the *Mahābhārata* 112.58.13). It is through *utthāna* that Indra and the gods obtained *svarga loka* (the *Mahābhārata* 112.58.14).

The *Arthaśāstra* of Kauṭilya fully supports this idea of *artha*. It declares in 1.19.35: *arthasya mūla utthānam*: effort is the basis of all wealth or prosperity.[9] Again, in 15.1.1. it is said: *manuṣyāṇām vṛttirarthaḥ*: *artha* is the source of livelihood of human beings.

The second source of *artha* is manual skill. *Siddhārtha* (success or achievement) is based on the use of the hands (*paṇyah*), that is skill. There is no source of gain or profit superior to manual skill: *na pāṇilābhādadhiko lābhaḥ kascaṇa vidyate*.

The classes which create wealth

The sources of vitality of a people (*lokasya jīvanam*) are agriculture (*kṛṣī*), cow protection (*goraksā* or animal husbandry), trade and business (*vāṇijya*, *vāoiya*), according the *Mahābhārata* 3.198.23. To these Śāntiparva (the *Mahābhārata* 12.161.10 and 31) adds *śilpa* (handicrafts) and *kārakaḥ* (skilled workmen). *Manusmṛti* 10.116 enumerates more less the same professions as sources of wealth.

Thus, it is the Vaiśya and the lower castes of craftsmen and workers who are directly engaged in production, who create wealth. The Brāhmaṇas, who are engaged in caste professions like imparting education, performing of religious ceremonies, etc. and the Kṣatriyas, who are engaged in maintaining law and order and external security, contribute to production only indirectly by creating conditions for the development of mental faculties and the conditions of security.

Ingredients of artha

Artha excludes wealth or property acquired illegally through theft, cheating, through foul or unfair means such as cheating, tax evasion, or exploitation. This is so, because such *artha* will have been acquired by conduct and activity in conflict with, or rather contrary to, *dharma*. This is *artha dūṣanam*, tainted wealth, of *Manusmṛti* 6.48. Sāyaṇa in his *Puruṣārathasudhānidhi* 2.7 quotes a verse from the Mahābhārata: *anyāyenārjitam drvyamarthadūṣaṇamucyati*; property acquired by in fair means is tainted. So in the *Mahābhārata* 12.254.6 Tulādhāra emphasizes that a person should live by such activity for gathering *artha* as is consistent with true *dharma* (*ya vṛttiḥ sa paro dharmastena jīvamī*) and by activity which does not cause harm, injury including deception and cheating to other beings (*adroheṇa bhūtānām*); without an intention of unlawful gain to himself or unlawful loss to another (*iṣṭa aniṣṭa-vimuktaḥ*); abandoning all desire for undue gain (*prātirāga bahiṣkṛta*) and, therefore, whose dealings are just and fair like the weighing balance (*tulā*). The *Mahābhārata* 5.122.04 warns that, if a person, out of greed, discards *dharma* (*lobhādharmam vipro jahati*) he is destroyed by the illicit and unfair means used (*anupayeṇa*)[10] to achieve *kāma* and *artha*.

The test of legitimate *artha* is to be found in whether it is fit for being given as *dāna* or for performing yajña. Only such property can be given as a gift which has been acquired justly and is also self-acquired. The *Mahābhārata* 13.113.22-23 speaks of donation of grain gathered by fair means: *nyāyenānnapārjitam*. In the Asvamedhikaparvan, it is laid down that that *dāna* (gift) is untainted which is given out of wealth or property acquired justly (*nyāyopāttena*, The *Mahābhārata* 14.93.57; *nyayālabdhai*, the *Mahābhārata* 14.93.73; *yathā-nyāyena sancitai*, the *Mahābhārata* 14.93.76; *and nyāya vṛtti*, The *Mahābhārata* 14.93.77). Agastya in the *Mahābhārata* 3.96.4 and 15 asks for only so much of wealth as is within the capacity of the donor and does not cause harm or damage to anyone (*yatha saktya vihiṁsyānyāsam vibhāgam prayacca me*).

The *Mahābhārata* 3.245.32 stresses that the *dāna* of wealth acquired unjustly (*anyāya śamupāttena*) does not free the donors from future dangers. The *Mahābhārata* 14.14.23 makes it clear that *yajña* performed with *anyayaparjita dhana*, wealth acquired unjustly, does not bear fruit. This is also the purport of *anyāyenārtha sañcayān* in the *Mahābhārata* 6.38.12.

Again, the untainted gift must be from self-acquired property (*yatnataḥ*, the *Mahābhārata* 14.93.57): *svaśaktya svārjitam*, the *Mahābhārata* 14.93.76). So the *Mahābhārata* proclaims that a donor who gifts someone else's property goes to hell (*datvā sa pārkyam narakam samavāptavān*, the *Mahābhārata* 14.93.74). Thus, the tests of untainted property[11] fit for *dāna* are two: having been honestly acquired and self-acquired.[12] It is this teaching of the *Mahābhārata* which becomes the basis for Devāla's (A.D. 600-900)[13] injunction that a gift must have been acquired by the donor in a proper way, that is, by the donor himself (*svayam arjitam*) and without having caused pain or loss to another (*aparābādham kleśam*).

Thus, *artha* excludes property acquired illegally or unfairly In my opinion, it would also exclude excessive wealth; as such wealth is unlikely to have been acquired by legitimate means or by personal efforts. More importantly, excessive wealth leads to concentration of economic power in the hands of the holder of the property, and leads inherently to the unfair and unjust relationship and use of property. In short, any wealth or property acquired by *adhārmic* means or which leads to *adhārmic* conduct is not *artha*.

It is significant that in Hindu mythology *artha* is the son of *dharma* and *buddhi*.

WHAT IS *kāma*?

Kāma[14] means wish, desire, longing, love, affection, pleasure, enjoyment, love, especially sexual love, carnal gratification, lust. Here it is appropriate to notice the peculiar features of *kāma*. *Kāma* grows by indulgence; the more one indulges in desires and sense enjoyment, the more it whets the appetite of the senses.

Sense enjoyment does not bring about fulfilment as happens in the case of acquisition of *artha*. As *Manusmṛti* 2.94 explains:[15] *na jātu kāmaḥ kāmānam upabhogena śāmyate*: desires are never appeased by their enjoyment or gratification. Secondly, *kāma* is blind. It is, therefore, absolutely essential that *kāma* is regulated by *dharma*. The stage of the householder (*gṛhastha āśrama*), according to *dharma*, provides one of the means for the healthy exercise of the *puruṣartha* of *kāma*. Further, in the context of the *puruṣārthas*, we feel that *kāma* has a limited, somewhat specialized meaning. We would call it 'the biological motivating force' having a twofold purpose: preservation and perpetuation.

If individuals have to live their full span of life, it is essential that their bodily needs—food, drink, clothing and shelter—must be met adequately. *Kāma* is, first, the motivating force for acquiring the *artha* necessary for essential bodily survival needs. It is in this sense that *Bṛhadāraṇyaka Upaniṣad* 4.4.5 explains *kāma*.

Again, all beings, or rather all organisms, cling to life tenaciously and wish to prolong it indefinitely. In other words, no organism wants to die, in fact, it wants freedom from death, it aspires for immortality. This is a fundamental psychological characteristic of all organic life. This is the second aspect of *kāma*, the biological motivating force for existence.

The death of all organisms, however, is inherent in the constitution of this universe and hence inescapable. Since the deathlessness or immortality of a particular organism is impossible, it seeks immortality through progeny, through reproduction. It thereby achieves immortality not of the individual but of the species. *Kāma* or sex is thus the means of perpetuating the species and fulfils the fundamental psychological urge for immortality through reproduction, through progeny, which we would call immortality via a proxy. In the context of the *puruṣārathas*, *kāma* is not *bhog*. *Kāma* (sex) is not sexual indulgence but sexual activity essential for immortality through perpetuation of the species. Sexual indulgence and promiscuity will be *adhārmic* being both harmful to the organism and unjustified by the needs of the species. We have earlier explained that the *artha* for fulfilment of *kāma* through the preservation of an organism must also be acquired in accordance with *dharma*. Hence Kṛṣṇa in the *Bhagavadgītā* 7.11.

declares: *dharmaviruddho bhūteṣu kāmo'smi*; I am *kāma* in conformity with *dharma*.

Even if the term *kāma* were to be interpreted in the general sense of desire, the desire must be regulated or controlled by *dharma*. Desires or wants are otherwise unlimited. Again, persons can be extremely selfish in pursuit of their desires. Thus, uncontrolled pursuit of unlimited individual wants and selfish desires can lead to conflict in society and to its disintegration. *Tṛṣṇā* (craving) is the antithesis of *lokasaṁgraha*. Hence the need for *tṛṣṇā nirodha* (suppression of craving) through *dharma*. It is significant that in Hindu mythology *kāma* is the son of Dharma and Śraddhā or Laksmi.

WHAT IS *mokṣa*?

Mokṣa[16] means emancipation, liberation, release; release from wordly existence or transmigration; final or eternal emancipation; *nirvāṇa, kaivalya*. In the context of *puruṣarthas*, the fourth aim of *mokṣa* is usually interpreted as connoting transcendental liberation, freedom from rebirth and hence freedom from the continued worldly existence of an individual *ātmā* or soul. According to the classical doctrine of *karma, karma* means bondage. Good *karma* may lead to rebirth in better and higher states of existence but not *mokṣa*. A person who has been engaged in *artha* and *kāma* for the better part of his life cannot hope to win *mokṣa* till all his *sañcita karmas* are exhausted. And the activities in pursuit of *artha* and *kāma* can only result in continuous piling up of *sañcita karmas*. More importantly, in our opinion, *mokṣa*, which is supposed to end the transmigrating process—*punarjanma* or rebirth—is a wholly impracticable ideal. It seeks to bring the universe, the life process, to a halt. We, therefore, feel that the only rational meaning of *mokṣa* could be freedom from desire, *tṛṣṇā* or *kāma*, *tṛṣṇa nirodha*. A person who has led a full life, has been engaged in meaningful economic activity, has reared a family, and no longer needs to or has the physical strength to undertake economic activity; whose sexual power is on the decline, and who has practised *dharma* in the near future should cultivate detachment, *vairāgya, anāṣakti yoga*.[17] In the third and fourth *aśramas*, detachment renunciation of wants and curbing of desires alone can give him happiness and obviate frustrations inevitable in pursuit of *artha* and *kāma*. The ideal of *mokṣa* is *jīvanmukti*. Thus *mokṣa*, in the context of the *puruṣarthas*, means renouncing secular activities, entering the fourth *āśrama*, and leading a life free from attachment and desires. It is the antithesis of *artha* and *kāma*.

Relationship between dharma, artha and kāma

The *Mahābhārata* 12.123.4 proclaims that *dharma* is the root (dharma *mūlastu*), *artha* is the body or trunk (*dehosṛthaḥ*) and *kāma* is the fruit of *artha* (*kāma artha phalam*). The *Mahābhārata* 12.161.2 asserts that *dharme cārthe ca kāme ca lokavṛttih samāhitā*; *dharma, artha, kāma* regulate the smooth functioning of society. *Artha* is the essential limb or component (*avayava*) of *dharma* and *kāma*, and only after the attainment of *artha* (*artha siddhyā*) can the other two (*dharma* and *kāma*) be developed and accomplished: (*nirvṛttāvubhāvetau*, the *Mahābhārata* 12.161.13). *Artha* alone determines the scope of *karmas* (including performance of rituals); without *artha*, *ṛta* or *dharma* cannot exist (*na ṛte arthena* (*vartate*), and *dharma* and *kāma* cannot subsist *dharma kāmāvita*, the *Mahābhārata* 12.161.13). The *Mahābhārata* 12.251.3 makes *artha* the fourth *lakṣaṇa*, the distinguishing characteristic of *dharma*, the other three being *sadācāra*, Smṛti and Veda.

Naturally, the *Mahābhārata* 12.161.23 advises that *artha* should be coupled with *dharma* (*artho dharmeṇa saṁyukto* and vice versa). On the other hand, if a person obtains wealth by unfair means (*anartha*), he cannot achieve *kāma* (*anarthasya na kāmossti*), and an unjust person (*adharmiṇaḥ*) cannot obtain *artha* (the *Mahābhārata* 12.161.24). It is only by imparting *dharma* (*dharma pradānena*), that is, by adhering to *dharma*, that a person achieves fulfilment (*sadhyosrthaḥ*). For obtaining *artha* coupled with *dharma* (*artham dharrasanyuktam*), it is an essential precondition that he must observe *dharma* (*dharmam samācareta pūrvam*, the *Mahābhārata* 12.161.24-26).[18] No wonder, the *Mahābhārata* 12.8.17[19] and 12.8.21[20] say that *dharma* and *kāma*, cannot be attained or completed without *artha*.

The regulation of *artha* and *kāma* by *dharma* is also important from the religious point of view. It is essential for man to undertake activity (*kriyā*) for achieving the goals of *artha* and *kāma*. Such *kriyā* must necessarily involve moral actions, *karma*. Consequently, if the *karma* done in pursuit of *artha* and *kāma* are not good (*punya*) but evil (*pāpa*), it is bound to compromise the future of the soul (*puruṣa*) responsible for those acts. So *dharma* is essential not only from the practical point of view in this life but also from the metaphysical angle.

There is a conflict between the *trivarga* of the *Mahābhārata* and Kauṭilya's *Arthaśāstra*. In the order of enumeration of the *trivarga puruṣarthas* in the *Mahābhārata* (1.56.33 and 12.123.4),[21] *dharma* is the foremost followed by *artha* and *kāma*. In the *Arthaśāstra*, on the other hand, *artha* precedes *dharma* with *kāma* occupying the third place. *Arthaśāstra* 9.7.61 specifically directs that the pursuit of goals should be in the order mentioned, viz. *artha* followed by *dharma* and *kāma*.

Again, *Arthaśāstra* 1.7.6-7 declares *artha* as the root (*mūla*) of *dharma* and *kāma*. But in the *Mahābhārata* 12.123.4 *dharma* is declared to be the root (*mūla*) of all the *arthas*. The *Mahābhārata* 5.124.34-47emphasizes that, if we cannot attain all the three goals, then the two goals, *dharma* and *artha* have to be pursued and if only one is attainable, then only *dharma*, and that only fools consider *kāma* as the supreme *puruṣārtha*. The *Mahābhārata* 12.92.48 declares that *dharma* is superior (*uttaro*) among the three.

It is evident that there was a shift between the *Arthaśāstra* of Kautilya and the *Mahābhārata* regarding the relative importance and role of the three *arthas*.

CRITICISM OF THE DOCTRINE OF THE *puruṣārthas* BY MODERN SCHOLARS AND ITS VALIDITY

The most important criticism of the doctrine of the *puruṣārthas* is that the *puruṣārthas* lack in content mainly project the goal of man in general terms. It is emphasized that the original sources do not give any detailed treatment[22] of the *puruṣārthas*. The theory of *dharma* or even the theory of *puruṣārthas* itself (*trivarga* and *caturvarga*) seems to do well as a theory of human goals only as long as goals are stated in general terms such as *artha*, *kāma*, *dharma*, etc. But difficulties start creeping in as soon as an attempt is made to give concrete content to these values, i.e. to state which specific things are to be sought or preferred to which other, and in what circumstances.[23] Another scholar has gone to the extent of asserting that the *puruṣārthas* are myths: *dharma* is not defined; it is not clear what *dharma* is: '...there are no *śāstras* to tell us how to pursue *artha* as a *puruṣārtha* in the sense of wealth unless all the diverse methods of cheating the State described in the *Arthaśāstra* are treated as such.'[24]

We have cited textual evidence from the *Mahābhārata* which clearly shows that the criticism is not justified. There is a reasonably adequate exposition of *dharma* and of the contents of the *puruṣārthas*, especially *dharma* and *artha*.

The general story of the *Mahābhārata* also leaves no scope for doubt as to what a person's *dharma* is in a particular situation: the Pāṇḍavas went to war to fulfil their obligation to *dharma* to enforce their just and rightful claim to property and the throne. Yudhiṣṭhira delays the regaining of his lost throne, because he will not break his solemn promise to shorten the period of exile and win back the lost kingdom, even though he had the power to do so. Dharmarāja spurns the happiness of wealth and power to be acquired through unrighteousness: *nahām nikṛtyā kāmaye sukhany uta dhanāni vā*: I do not desire for happiness and wealth obtained by unfair means (the *Mahābhārata* 2.53.10).

In the supreme crises of war, Kṛṣṇa shows the path of duty to Arjuna and dispels his doubts. In the face of this, it cannot be maintained that the scope and content of *dharma* as a *puruṣārtha* are not ascertainable.

Another controversy raised by modern scholars is whether there is conflict between *mokṣa*, the fourth *puruṣārtha*, and the first three goals, *dharma*, *artha* and *kāma*. This controversy arises from the classification of the *puruṣārthas*; the first three *puruṣārthas* are regarded as socially functional, whereas *mokṣa* is regarded as exclusively personalistic, individualistic, and socially non-functional; so it is thought that 'the theory of *puruṣārthas* is not made richer or more complete and exhaustive' by the addition of *mokṣa* as the fourth *puruṣārtha*. It converts, rather debases, the social ethics of *trivarga* into a personalistic social ethic. In the words of the critic: to make *dharma* itself a means to *mokṣa* amounts to subverting this entire scheme of life as it amounts to making *dharma* a means to (personal) salvation.[25]

Again, after reaching *mokṣa* a person ceases to be socially relevant; he ceases to be a social creature, the pursuit of *mokṣa* is, therefore, held to weaken [the] 'sanctity of morality'.[26] This is reinforced by the fact that in *mokṣa* the distinction between good and evil, between right and wrong disappears.

Another scholar has observed that *mokṣa* transcends both *dharma* and *kāma*, and thus occupies an anomalous position among the *puruṣārthas*. It is not clear whether transcendence should be understood as a negation or fulfilment of other *puruṣārthas*.[27] He goes on to observe: '... the radical difference between *mokṣa* as a *puruṣāratha* and the other three *puruṣārathas* has not only to be recognized ... but also the radical incompatibility between them at least in the direction to which their seeking would lead.'[28] To him, therefore, *mokṣa* is tangential to all other *puruṣārathas*.

We feel that these criticisms of the doctrine of *puruṣārtha*, especially of the role of *mokṣa* are factually incorrect. The *puruṣārtha* of *mokṣa* does not lead to indifference to surroundings or to social problems. The ideal of *mokṣa* could be both personalistic and universalistic. A person on attaining enlightenment, but before his *mahāparinirvāṇa*, that is, when he is on the threshold of *mokṣa*, no longer pursues personalistic *artha* and *kāma*, he does not act for his own personal benefit. But he is not dysfunctional or inactive. He is devoid of selfish *kāma*. He engages himself in intense but socially beneficial impersonal activity like a *bodhisattva*. His *artha* and *kāma* are sublimated and are no longer personalistic but universalistic. This ideal of intense altruistic activity is embodied in the *bodhisattva* ideal. Ramakrishna in the nineteenth century had warned Vivekananda against cultivating *nirvikalpa samādhi* to attain identity with the absolute on the ground that it was a form of pleasure forbidden to those noble souls whose duty it was to sacrifice their own happiness in the service of others.[29] Again, Ramakrishna had himself prayed to Mother: 'O Mother let me remain in contact with man. Do not make me a dried up ascetic.' The Mother replied: 'Stay on the threshold of relative consciousness for the love of humanity.'

Detachment and *mokṣa* do not mean indifference. *Niṣkāmakarma* does not mean cessation of activity: it means *karma* without selfish, personal interest. It is the basis of the intense altruistic activity of a *karmayogī* of the *Bhagavadgītā* and of a Vimalakīrti of the *Vimalakīrti-nirdeśa*. Further, the manner in which we have interpreted *mokṣa* eliminates the alleged conflict between *mokṣa* and the first three *puruṣārthas.*

Some modern scholars assert that the scheme of values embodied in the *puruṣārthas* is hierarchical with *mokṣa* in the *caturvarga* and *kāma* in the *trivarga* being the *paramapuruṣārtha,* the apex[30] of the goals. The terms 'hierarchy' and 'hierarchical' are obviously being used to convey an arrangement of values in a graduated series, the different values being placed in a series in accordance with their relative importance or degree of perfection. On this basis, *mokṣa* is at the apex and *artha* or *kāma* at the bottom.

It appears that the concept of a hierarchy in the *puruṣārathas* has been evolved with reference to their classification as intrinsic or end values and instrumental or means values, and this has been briefly referred to earlier. On this basis, in the *trivarga, kāma* will be the end value, and *dharma* and *artha* instrumental values; in the *caturvarga, mokṣa* is the end value, and the other three *puruṣārathas* are instrumental values. End values are ranked higher than means or instrumental values.

Traditionally, *dharma* and *mokṣa* are considered as *alaukika* or spiritual values as distinct from the *laukika* or mundane values, *artha* and *kāma.* In the context of ends and means values, this leads to an anomaly; a spiritual or *alaukika* value, viz. *dharma,* helps in the attainment of a *laukika* or mundane value, viz. *kāma.* Again, without *artha,* neither *kāma* nor *dharma* can subsist; *artha* is their essential limb. *Artha* is vital for the fulfilment of *kāma* and the growth of *dharma.* Again, *kāma* is equally fundamental; it is the will to live. It is with reference to this will that *dharma* and *artha* find fulfilment. If there be lack of will to live (*kāma*) or of the means to live (*artha*), there cannot be any *puruṣārtha.*

Also the importance of a particular *puruṣārtha* varies with the stage of life, the *āśrama,* in which a man is in, during the course of his life's journey. In the *brahmacarya āśrama, dharma* is of utmost importance with minimal *artha* and *kāma* essential for bodily maintenance. In the *gṛhastha āśrama, kāma* is of paramount importance, but it must be adequately supported by *artha* and tempered by *dharma.* In the *sannyāsa āśrama, mokṣa* coupled with *dharma* is the *paramapuruṣārtha, artha* and *kāma* playing a minimal role. In fact, one *puruṣārtha* becomes the foundation of either one or two *puruṣārthas* depending upon the stage of life (*āśrama*) of the person concerned. In other words, the scheme of the *puruṣārthas* ceases to be hierarchical.[31]

While *artha* is the means to live and *kāma* is the will to live, *dharma* provides the disciplinary and regulatory milieu and the ideological inspiration for their healthy pursuit and fulfilment. In fact, *dharma* is essential for *lokasaṁgraha*, an integrated society in which alone *artha* and *kāma* can be pursued meaningfully. From this point of view, there is no hierarchy among the *puruṣārthas*. Each of the *puruṣārthas* is interrelated with the others.[32]

NOTES

1. The *Mahābhārata* 5.122.32; 12.59.30, etc. *Manusmṛti* 2.224; Kauṭilya's *Arthasāśtra* 9.7.60. *Amarakoṣa* 2.7.57.
2. Cited by P.V. Kane in *History of Dharmaśāstras*, vol. 1 pt. 1, p. 4, fn. 12, Pune, 1968.
3. *Yatosbhyudaya niḥsreyasasiddhiḥ sa dharmaḥ Vaiśeṣika Sutra* 1.2.
4. *Mīmāṁsānyāyaprakāśa* 3, cited by V.S. Sukthankar in *On the Meaning of the Mahābhārata*, Bombay, 1957, p. 79.
5. *Dharmaśabdaḥ kartavyatā vacanaḥ*.
6. *Upāyam dharmamevāhustrīvargasya*—the *Mahābhārata* 5.122.36.
7. Kauṭilya in his *Arthaśāstra* 1.7 recognizes *dharmārthāvirodhena kāmam seveta* (a person may enjoy *kāma* if there is no conflict between *dharma* and *artha*). Again, *Manusmṛti* 4.176 declares: *parityajedar-thakāmau yau syātām dharma varjitau* (devoid of *dharma*, *artha* and *kāma* have to be abandoned or given up).
8. Monier-Williams, *Sanskrit-English Dictionary;* V.S. Apte, *Sanskrit-English Dictionary*.
9. *Arthaśāstra* 1.19.36 says: *aṇutthāne dhruvo nāsah prāptasyānagatasya ca/ Prāpyate phalamutthānāllabhate cārthasampadam//*. In the absence of effort, decay will follow what has been gained, and what is still to be acquired. It is through effort that one gets the fruits of action and wealth.
10. *Manusmṛti* 4.15 also condemns acquisition of wealth by conspiracy (*prasangena*) or by prohibited act, (*nehetārthān prasangena viruddhena Karmanā*). *Manusmṛti* 5.106 says that honestly acquired *artha* makes a person pure: *yo arthe suchir sa sucinar* and not earth and water.
11. *Manusmṛti* 4.226 calls it *svāgatadhana*.
12. The *Mahābhārata* 3.200.59 (Bombay ed.) declares that *dāna* is futile *inter alia* if it is given from wealth that has been earned wrongly. See P.C. Roy's translation of the *Mahābhārata*.
13. Quoted from P.V. Kane, *History of the Dharmaśāstrās* vol. ii, pt. ii. Pune, 1974, p. 847, fn 1999.

14. See Monier-Williams and also V.S. Apte, *Sanskrit-English Dictionary*.
15. See also Ādiparvan of the *Mahābhārata* (cr. ed.) 1.70.41 n. 693 and 1.80.7 n. 840.
16. See Monier-Williams, *Sanskrit-English Dictionary* and also V.S. Apte, *Sanskrit-English Dictionary*.
17. We feel that, in the *Sannyāsdharma Viṣaya* of *Manusmṛti* 6.35-37, Manu speaks of *mokṣa* in the sense of the fourth *āśrama, sannyāsa*, renunciation of secular life, and not of the final emancipation, *nirvāṇa*, from the life process. Two courses are further open to a person who becomes a *saññyāsī*: either he can work for the attainment of release from the bondage of *karma* (*karmabhirṇa nibadhyate, Mausmṛti* 6.74) and attains release from transmigration (*Manusmṛti* 6.79, 81 and 85); or remains in this world and attains eternal happiness here and in the world to which he goes hereafter (*pretya, Manusmṛti* 6.74 and 80). An *ajñāna saññyāsī* attains only heaven (*svarga, Manusmṛti* 6.84).
18. *Manusmṛti* 4.176 advises discarding that *artha* and *kāma* which have been condemned by *dharma* (see note 7).
19. *arthāddharmasca kāmasca, svargasca prāṇayātrā na prasidhyati.*
20. *Dharma, kāma, śvarga, arthat sarvaṇipravartante.*
21. *Manusmṛti* 2.224 follows the same sequence of *puruṣārthas*.
22. Rajendra Prasad, 'Theory of *Puruṣārthas*: Revaluation and Reconstruction' in *Journal of Indian Philosophy*, Dodrecht, Holland, 1981, p. 50. According to R.N. Dandekar, 'The whole theory of *puruṣārthas* suffers from the lack of a logically argued and analytically defended treatment.' See 'The Theory of *Puruṣārthas*: 'Rethinking' in *Annals B.O.R.I.*, vol. lxviii, Pune, 1987, pp. 667-68.
23. Rajendra Prasad, *ibid.*, p. 62.
24. Daya Krishna, 'The Myth of *Puruṣārthas*' in *Journal of Indian Council of Philosophical Research*, vol. iv, no. 1, 1986, pp. 10, 11, 13.
25. Rajendra Prasad, *ibid.*, pp. 68, 69. He adds: 'The addition of *mokṣa* does not seem to fill in or improve upon the theory of *trivarga* from the point of view of offering a descriptive-cum-prescriptive picture of how best social life [should] be organised and regulated.' *Ibid.*, p. 66.
26. Rajendra Prasad, *ibid.*, p. 69.
27. Daya Krishna, op. cit., p. 6.
28. *Ibid.*, pp. 6 and 7. Dandekar in his 'The Theory of *Puruṣārthas*: A Rethinking', *ibid.*, pp. 664-67 makes similar observations: *mokṣa* falls outside the orbit of the social-functional theory of the *puruṣārthas* that there is conceptual disparity and discontinuity between the *trivarga* and *mokṣa*; *mokṣa* implies transcending the phenomenal world; *mokṣa* means release from the continued embodied existence, the isolation of the soul from non-soul; *mokṣa* is personalistic and not social. *Mokṣa* thus forms a sharp dichotomy with the other three *puruṣārthas*, particularly with *dharma*. While *dharma* aims at the maintenance of the world order, *mokṣa* deliberately rejects it. The purport of *mokṣa* is the negation of *dharma*.
29. Romain Rolland, *Prophets of New India*, London, 1930, p. 56. When

young Naren begged him to open to him the *nirvikalpa samādhi*, the terrible door leading to the gulf of the Absolute, Ramakrishna refused and was angry. 'Shame on you', he cried, 'I thought you were to be the great banyan tree giving shelter to thousands of tired souls. Instead you are selfishly seeking your own wellbeing. ...'

30. '...the fourth element completes, encompasses and transcends the first three, at the same time as expressing their quintessence.' Charles Malamoud, 'On the Rhetoric and Semantics of *Puruṣārthas*' in *Way of Life*, ed. T.N. Madan, New Delhi, 1982, p. 37.

31. Charles Malamoud in his article 'On the Rhetoric and Semantics of *Puruṣārtha*', *vide* T.N. Madan (ed.), *Way of Life*, pp. 41 and 42 calls it a 'revolving hierarchy' of the *puruṣārthas*. He justifies this with reference to the differences of opinion in the texts regarding the relative place of the various *puruṣārthas*, and the multiplicity of points of view regarding their interrelationship. We submit that a 'revolving hierarchy' is a contradiction in terms for it ceases to be hierarchical once it is revolving or cyclical.

32. According to *Manusmṛti* 6.36-37, 'If a man desires *mokṣa* without having performed these duties (study of the Veda, producing sons and performing religious sacrifices), he falls into hell.'

THE SOCIO-MORAL IMPLICATIONS OF DRAUPADĪ'S MARRIAGE TO FIVE HUSBANDS

A.N. JANI

EVERY society, whether primitive or literate, has its own rules of morality. Society is expected to adhere to them scrupulously so as to uphold society. A breach of the moral laws proves detrimental to the welfare and unity of society. Certain values such as truth, non-violence, etc. are universal, while others may change from society to society and according to the special needs of times and climes.

The *Mahābhārata*, which is not only a historical heroic poem (*itihāsa*) but also a book on law and morals (*dharmaśāstra*), on ethics (*nīti*), in fact, an encyclopaedia of Indian culture, presents a variety of moral dilemmas. One of these is the account of Draupadī's marriage to five husbands. This is the solitary instance of polyandrous marriage in the national epic of India. The problem of Draupadī's marriage is introduced in chap. 191 (182)* of the Ādiparvan. When Bhīma and Arjuna returned to their residence from the *svayaṃvara* of Draupadī in which Arjuna proved victorious in the most difficult test of piercing the fish and won Draupadī as his wife, they introduced Draupadī as 'alms' to their mother Kuntī, who, without looking at the 'alms', told them to enjoy it jointly. But soon, on seeing Draupadī, she realized what a great blunder she had committed in asking them to enjoy the 'alms' jointly. She turned to Yudhiṣṭhira, the embodiment of *dharma*, to find out some way so that, on the one hand, her words might not prove false, and, on the other, Draupadī be free from

*Figure in brackets indicate the no. of the chapter in the critical edition.

committing an *adharma*.[1] Yudhiṣṭhira pronounced an impartial judgement, and told Arjuna: 'You have won this lady, and therefore, you are the proper person to marry her.'[2] But Arjuna hesitated on the ground that he would not like to marry as long as his two elder brothers, namely, Yudhiṣṭhira and Bhīma, are unmarried.

In the meantime, however, clever Yudhiṣṭhira noticed that Draupadī's extraordinary beauty had generated in all of them (even in him) an irresistible passion. The foresighted Yudhiṣṭhira thought that Draupadī's marriage with Arjuna or anyone of them would create discord in the unity and harmony of the five brothers, so in order to avoid such a situation, Yudhiṣṭhira pronounced his judgement: 'This Draupadī shall be a common wife of all of us.'[3] Thus, on the one hand, he tried to make Kuntī's words true; and, on the other, avoided disastrous envy among themselves under the pretext of obeying the words of the mother who is a most revered person. But this fantastic solution is far from satisfactory. It is difficult to believe that a casual command of Kuntī could be obeyed so literally. It is also likely that Kuntī might not have said what she is reckoned to say.

When Drupada, after knowing the identity of the Pāṇḍavas, approached Yudhiṣṭhira with a proposal to celebrate Draupadī's marriage with Arjuna, the latter said: 'Arrange for my marriage also.' To this the king said: 'Then Yudhiṣṭhira! You may marry my daughter or you may suggest the name of anyone of your brothers. I shall marry her to him.' Yudhiṣṭhira said: 'Draupadī should be the common wife of us all as by the command of our mother. As long as Bhīma and I are unmarried, Arjuna cannot marry. Again, we all have decided to enjoy collectively any excellent thing we get. Therefore, Draupadī should marry all five of us one by one.'[4]

Flabbergasted at such a proposal, the king reproachfully said to Yudhiṣṭhira: 'To one man many wives are ordained. But it is never heard that one woman should have many husbands. You know the law and justice. Therefore, you should not utter such an unlawful statement which is against the Vedic as well as popular conventions. Fie upon your intelligence.'[5] But these words had no effect on Yudhiṣṭhira. He replied: 'It is difficult to decide what is *dharma* and what is *adharma*. It is very subtle and its real implication is beyond our ken to grasp. *Here we simply follow the path trodden by our ancestors.* Our mother also desires this. Therefore, oh king! honour this *dharma* without doubting it any more.'[6]

The ingenious redactor of the *Mahābhārata* cleverly bring in [196 (188)] Vyāsa at this juncture to solve the puzzling issue. Drupada expressed his displeasure to the proposal of Yudhiṣṭhira before him. Draupadī's brother Dhṛṣṭadyumna also opposed it bitterly, saying: 'How can an elder brother behave wickedly and enjoy the wife of his younger brother?'[7] Yudhiṣṭhira, in order to prove the legality of his proposal, quoted two precedents from the past, that of Jaṭilā who married seven sages and that of Vārkṣī, who married ten brothers known as Pracetases.[8] Secondly, he repeated Kuntīs command to enjoy the 'alms' jointly. Kuntī corroborated his view by saying that what Yudhiṣṭhira, the follower of *dharma*, says is completely true.[9]

On hearing the pros and cons of the problem, Vyāsa pronounced the judgement: 'What Yudhiṣṭhira says is, no doubt, *dharma*. Draupadī is ordained to be the wife of five husbands. It is not at all censurable.'[10] To justify the polyandrous marriage of Draupadī, Vyāsa quotes two fantastic stories about the previous birth of Draupadī and the Pāṇḍavas. According to the first story, a beautiful but unlucky daughter of a sage practised penance and propitiated Śiva who appeared before her. She impatiently asked five times for a husband. Lord Śiva, therefore, granted her five husbands in the next birth. Vyāsa then said to Drupada that the same girl was born as his daughter, and, therefore, her marriage with five Pāṇḍavas was inevitable and uncensurable, being a boon of Lord Śiva.[11]

Another Saivite story known as Pāncendropākhyāna narrates 'how Indra, as a penalty for having insulted Śiva, is divided into five parts and is born on the earth; and an incarnation of Lakṣmī is determined to be his wife'.[12]

Thus, it was proved that the five Pāṇḍava brothers were incarnations of *one* Indra and Draupadī, who represented Lakṣmi, would therefore, actually have one husband in spite of her apparent marriage with five.[13]

There is a contradiction in both the above stories. The first one tries to justify Draupadī's marriage with five husbands on the ground of such a boon from Śiva, while the second story tries to prove that the Pāṇḍavas been five parts of one Indra, Draupadī had, in fact, only one husband.

The Jain and Bauddha versions of the *svayaṁvara* of Draupadī make her choose not Arjuna only but all the five Pāṇḍavas at the same time.[14]

These stories reflect how the later redactors strove each in his own fanciful way to justify polyandrous marriage 'by means of many rather unskilfully inserted stories.'[15]

Some European scholars have also tried to justify the five-husband-marriage mythologically, allegorically, and symbolically.[16]

'There is not even an attempt made to reconcile these three stories of justification with one another or with the main story.'[17]

The real solution of the problem lies in the ethnological fact, recorded in Yudhiṣṭhira's intention that he is following the tradition of his ancestors. This sentence preserved from the old nucleus of the *Mahābhārata* shows that it was not a general Indian custom but only a particular typical custom prevailing in the family of the Pāṇḍavas. The custom of polyandry was prevalent in ancient times not only in India but in other countries such as North and South America, Africa, New Zealand and the pacific islands. In Tibet and the Himalayan region, it was an accepted custom. It prevailed in Śrī Lanka up to A.D. 1820 until the British Government declared it illegal. It prevails even today among the Toḍas of the Nilgiri Hills. Among the Nairs of Kerala[18] and in the northern part of Sikkim it is prevalent even today. This custom seems to have originated out of social necessity in those regions where the number of females was less than that of males. In some places, it came into existence with a view to keeping the family wealth in one place. Elsewhere it originated from the problem of protection of a woman whose husband was away from home for a very long time.[19] Thus, the custom originated out of the social and economical needs of the peoples concerned.

Originally, a woman was allowed to have sexual relations with persons not in any way related to her. Then such a marriage was restricted among the relatives, and then with the advent of time it must have been restricted among the brothers of the same family.[20]

The Pāṇḍavas were also brought from the Himalayas to the plains by sages, according to the *Mahābhārata* [ch. 126 (117)]. The custom of polyandry was in vogue in their family, as can be seen by Kuntī's having three sons from three different persons and Mādrī's having two sons from two other persons, at the repeated entreaties of Pāṇḍu[21] who was very anxious to beget children.

The custom of polyandry prevalent among certain tribes was, however, not approved by the civilized Aryans. Polyandry was never legalized by Indian law writers like Manu who approved of eight types of marriage and even of the levirate system. Drupada's hesitation and Dhṛṣṭadyumna's strong protest to Yudhiṣṭhira's proposal show that the Pāñcālas did not like this custom.

However, it is very strange that a spirited lady such as Draupadī kept quiet over a serious matter concerning her own life. It is likely that Draupadī and her father and brother must have been willing to accept polyandry. Perhaps Draupadī and her brother were of doubtful origin. They might have been forsaken children fostered by King Drupada or they might have been begotten by the Queen Pṛṣatī by levirate. Later on the story of their divine origin must have been fabricated to give them social sanction.[22] Similarly, the story of the divine origin of the Pāṇḍavas was also invented to give them an honourable status in the society. C.V. Vaidya rightly remarks that 'the Pāṇḍavas belonged to a family which was different from the Kuru family.'[23]

The Pāṇḍava family followed the primitive custom of polyandry which was looked down upon by the Kauravas and Pāñcālas. This indicates that there was a conflict between the moral codes followed by the Pāṇḍavas, on the one hand and the Kauravas and Pāñcālas, on the other. Efforts, therefore, were made by the later redactors of the *Mahābhārata* to solve these moral conflicts by inventing fanciful stories of the divine birth of Pāṇḍavas and Draupadī and by inventing unconvincing stories about the previous births of both the Pāṇḍavas and Draupadī to lessen the peculiarity of the polyandrous marriage.

C.V. Vaidya has suggested that this part of the narrative has reference to the second invasion of Aryan immigrants from the Himalaya region whose culture was different from that of early Aryan settlers. These later immigrants were later on accepted into their fold by the earlier settlers.[24]

NOTES

1. *Gatvā tu tāṁ Bhārgavakarmaśālāṁ*
Pārthau Pṛthāṁ prāpya māhānubhavau|
Tāṁ Yājñasenīṁ Paramapratītau
Bhikṣetyathāvedayatāṁ narāgrayau||
Kuṭīgatā sā tvanavekṣya putrau
Provāca bhuṅkteti sametya sarve|
Paścācca Kuntī prasamīkṣya kṛṣṇāṃ
Kaṣṭaṁ māya bhāṣitamityuvāca||
Mayā Kathaṁ nānṛtamuktamadya
Bhavet Kurūnāṁ ṛṣabha bravīhi|
Pancālarājasya sutāmadharmo
Na copavarteta na vibhramecca ||
—191(182)* 1-2, 5.

2. *Tvayā jitā Phālguna! Yājñasenī*
Tvayaiva śobhiṣyati rājaputrī |
Prajvālyatāmagniramitrasāha
Gṛhāṇa pāṇiṃ vidhivat tvamasyāḥ ||
—191(182)7.

3. *Teṣāṁ tu Draupadīṁ dṛṣṭvā sarveṣāmamitaujasām |*
Sampramathyendriyagrāmaṁ prādurāsīn manobhavah ||
Teṣāmākārābhāvajñaḥ Kuntīputro Yudhiṣṭhiraḥ |
Dvaipāyanavacaḥ kṛtsnaṁ sasmāra manujarṣabhaḥ ||

Abravīt sahitān bhrātṛn mitho bhedabhayān nṛpaḥ |
Sarveṣāṁ Draupadī bhāryā bhaviṣyati hi naḥ śubhā ||
—191(182)13, 15-16.

4. *Sarveṣāṁ mahiṣī rājan! Draupadī no bhaviṣyati|*
Evaṁ Pravyāhṛtaṃ pūrvaṁ mama mātrā viśāmpate!||
Eṣa naḥ samayo rājan! ratnasya sahabhojanam|
Na tu taṁ hātumicchāmaḥ samayaṁ rājasttama!||
—195(187)23, 25.

5. *Ekasya bahvyo viditā mahiṣyaḥ Kurunandana!|*
Naikasyā bahavah puṁsaḥ śrūyante patayaḥ kvacit||
Lokavedaviruddhaṃ tvaṁ nādharmaṁ dharmavic cuciḥ|
Kartumarhasi Kaunteya! kasmāt te buddhirīdṛśī||
—195(187) 27-28.

6. *Sūkṣmo dharmo mahārāja! nāsya vidmo vayaṁ gatim|*
Pūrveṣāmānupūrvyeṇa yātaṁ vartmānuyāmahe||
Na me vāganṛtaṃ prāha nādharme dhīyate matiḥ|
Evaṁ caiva vadantyambā mama caitan manogatam||
—195(187) 29-30.

7. *Yavīyasaḥ kathaṁ bhāryāṁ jyeṣṭho bhrātā dvijarṣabha!|*
Brahman! samabhivarteta savṛttaḥ sanstapodhana!||
—196 (188) 10.

*The figure in the bracket indicates the no. of ch. in the critical edition.

8. One more precedent of Śaibyā, the daughter of king Bhūmāśva, who married five sons of king Nitantu in a *svayaṃvara*, is recorded by C.R. Deshpande in *Transmission of the Mahābhārata Tradition*, Shimla, 1978, p. 110 from the *Mahābhārata* I. 101.D4.
9. *Evametad yathā prāha dharmacārī Yudhiṣṭhiraḥ//*

—196 (188)18.

10. *Yathā ca prāha Kaunteyastathā dharmo na saṁśayaḥ/*
Pañcānām vihitā patnī kṛṣṇā pārṣatyaninditā//

—196 (188)20.

11. *Āsīt tapovane kācid ṛṣeḥ kanyā mahātmanaḥ/*
Nādhyagacchat patiṁ sā tu Kanyā rūpavatī satī//
Atheśvaramuvācedam ātmanaḥ sā vaco hitam/
Patiṃ sarvaguṇopetam icchāmīti punaḥ punaḥ//
Tāmatha pratyuvācedamīśāṇo vadatāṁ varaḥ/
Pañca te patayaḥ śreṣṭhā bhaviṣyantīti Śaṅkaraḥ//
Pancakṛtvastvayā uktaḥ patiṁ dehītyahaṁ punaḥ/
Dehamanyaṁ gatāyāste yathoktaṁ tad bhaviṣyati//
Drupadaiṣā hi sā jajñe sutā te devarūpiṇī/
Pañcānāṁ vihitā patnī kṛṣṇā Pārṣatyaninditā//
Svargaśrīḥ Pāṇḍavārthāya samutpannā mahāmakhe/
Seha taptvā tapo ghoraṁ duhitṛtvaṁ tavāgatā//
Saiṣā devī rucirā devajuṣṭā
Pañcānāmekā svakṛtena Karmaṇā/
Sṛṣṭā svayaṃ devapatnī svayambhuvā
Śṛtvā rājan ! Drupadeṣṭaṁ kuruṣva//

—197 (189)43-49.

The same story is introduced earlier in ch. 169 (157), where Vyāsa advises Pāṇḍavas to reside in Pāñcāla city on the ground that their would-be-wife is already born there.
Last verses read as under:
Drupadasya kule jajñe sā kanyā devarūpiṇi/
Nirdiṣṭā bhavatāṁ patnī kṛṣṇā Pārṣatyaninditā//
Pāñcālanagare tasmān nivasadhvaṃ mahābalāḥ!//

—169 (157) 14-15.

12. M., Winternitz, *History of Indian Literature*, Delhi, 1981, p. 317, n. 1.
13. *Evamte Pāṇḍavāḥ sambabhūvur*
ye te rājan! pūrvamindrā babhūvuḥ/
Lakṣmīścaiṣāṁ pūrvamevopadiṣṭā
Bhāryā yaiṣā Draupadī divyarūpā//

—197(189)35

14. M. Winternitz, *Ibid.*
15. *Ibid.*
16. M., Winternitz, 'Notes on the *Mahābhārata*' JRAS, 1897, p. 733 ff.
17. ———, *History of Indian Literature*, vol. i., Delhi, 1981, p. 317, n. 1.
18. S.K. Pendse, *Mahābhāratātila Vyaktidarśana* (Marathi), Pune, 1964, pp. 237-38.
19. *Ibid.*

20. *Ibid.*
21. See the *Mahābhārata* I. 120 (111)-122 (113).
22. N.B. Patil, *The Folklore in the Mahābhārata*, 1983, pp. 106-07.
23. See *Epic India*, 1907, p. 14.
24. *Ibid.*

LA GUERRE DE KURUKṢETRA N'AURA PAS LIEU: UDYOGA RECONSIDERED

AMIYA DEV

I HAVE borrowed this title from Giraudoux for mere focus. My concern is with the Udyoga structure, with its interrelation of war preparations and peace efforts. I will restrict myself to three episodes: Kṛṣṇa's waking and Arjuna-Duryodhana's soliciting him for help at war (7: Poona ed.); Kṛṣṇa's peace mission (70-137); and Kṛṣṇa's overture to Karṇa (138-41). The first two are emblematic of war and peace; the third, I will argue, is a conjunct of war and peace. But since in considering Kurukṣetra I thought of Troy, let me open my discourse with a Homeric reference. It does have a distant, though indirect, parallel to the Udyoga situation. I am thinking of the first movement in *Iliad*, where the gods sit down to a meeting. The human war has come to a standstill. The Trojans and Achaeans had called a truce to let Paris and Menelaus fight it out between themselves. And in all probability the Achaeans would have secured victory, if Aphrodite, out of pity for her protégé, had not invisibly frisked him away from the battlefield. Anyway, since Paris was missing, the unfinished duel could surely be decided in Menelaus' favour, and the Achaeans could claim Helen. And Troy could be saved. It was at this juncture that the Olympians have met. Should they close the war or find some means to break the truce? Troy-lover Zeus is in favour of peace, but pro-Achaean Hera and Athena are dead against it. Such is their rancour against Troy that they do not seem impeded by the Achaean toll. Finally, Zeus yields to them, maybe because of immediate domestic peace or maybe because of a hint of destiny, though there is no clear evidence of that at this stage. Anyway, he yields only on the condition that whenever he wishes to sack any of Hera's favourite cities she must not demur. Thus the fate of Troy is sealed. Athena flashing down to the battlefield at Zeus' permission to work out the human detail—Pandarus shooting an arrow at Menelaus—strikes the Trojans and Achaeans with awe: 'Every man looked at his neighbour with a question on his lips', "Does this mean war again with all its horrors? Or is Zeus, our arbiter in battle, making peace between us?" (Penguin tr.)

As a human-divine pattern this looks quite simple; in fact, so simple that it may not be possible to read a Dumézilian myth-epic correspondence in this event. The Olympians, too, seem to be performing an epic action, as immediately motivated and temporally driven as Trojans and Achaeans. At least here, their action does not carry any cosmic significance. For instance, the dispute between Zeus and Hera on whether Troy should stay or go is too personal, almost like the dispute between Achilles and Agamemnon that opens the epic action in the *Iliad.* In any case, this simplicity is perhaps one reason why the Homeric poem is easier to approach. I remember I once had the temerity as a student, at the end of a guest lecture by the eminent Bruno Snell, to raise the issue of the *Mahābhārata* beside the *Iliad.* This was before Georges Dumézil and Madeleine Biardeau's momentous work was either published or publicized. The point is: the three episodes I have chosen from the Udyogaparvan are quite complex, the prime signifiers of that complexity being the 'ambiguity' around peace and the 'amphibian' role of Kṛṣṇa. For whatever the positivists may think—and I have Bankim in particular in mind—Kṛṣṇa's divinity is one of our basic *données*. But notwithstanding the magnitude of this divinity, it is obviously most unlike Zeus'. I suspect the subtler problem is as regards his humanity, for once you know him for a god, how are you going to take him for a man? (Maybe I am raising the wrong question through obvious acculturation, for the most ardent believers in Kṛṣṇa's divinity, Bhīṣma and Vidura, do not seem to have any problem at all. Anyway, I had also in mind the Hebrew and the Greek in Yeats' *Resurrection*, the former feeling it too much that a man, no matter how pure and how much of an idealist, should resuscitate, the latter thinking it unbelievable that a god's heart should beat.) Whichever it may be, humanity-heavy or divinity-heavy, Kṛṣṇa's 'amphibiousness' seems to be the primary issue here. But a direct probe may not be possible, and we may have to begin with the question of the ambiguity of war and peace.

There is no ambiguity about what Yudhiṣṭhira wants. Peace, but not to the extent of the total sacrifice of his rights. Similarly, there is no ambiguity about what his brothers, Draupadī, their allies like Drupada and Virāṭa and Sātyaki want, whether it is peace or war, a shade more or a shade less. After all, the Pāṇḍavas had a kingdom, and they have every reason to try to regain it since they have completed their term of exile. Yudhiṣṭhira says in so many words that a king without his kingdom is deficient in *dharma*, though he is also aware that war is a terrible affair and that victory in a war is tantamount to defeat. In a way, the Pāṇḍavas pass the ball to Duryodhana's court. If he admits their right and gives them back their kingdom, or even a part of it, they will have peace. It does not even cross their mind that this time too, as in the earlier event, after returning them their kingdom, Duryodhana may invite Yudhiṣṭhira to a fresh bout of dice. So, when Drupada advises them to send messengers to kings everywhere for alliance, they act accordingly. Their war preparations do not nullify their desire for peace. The embassy of Drupada's priest to the Kaurava court is, therefore, no diplomatic eyewash. But when it comes to Kṛṣṇa, their prime ally and their prime counsellor, we are not sure about his motive. Does he want war or does he want peace? This, I think, is the most insistent question of the Udyogaparvan.

If we look ahead to the Strīparvan and quote the instance of Gāndhārī's curse, then Kṛṣṇa's responsibility *in* the war is accepted. After all, he did let the two sides destroy each other. From there to retrospect to motivating the war is not much of a logical feat. If Kṛṣṇa could stay indifferent to Kuru-Pāṇḍava destruction, then Kṛṣṇa could also help cause that destruction. And, naturally if we add to Gāndhārī's curse the theophany on the battlefield, Kṛṣṇa manifesting himself to Arjuna as all-devouring destroyer Time, we have further indirect and retrospectively argued evidence for the war motivation. But retrospective arguing is structural and not narrative, and we are dealing with a narrative here in the Udyogaparvan, the narrative of Kṛṣṇa's simultaneous contribution to war preparations and peace overtures—our three episodes in other words.

Deconstructing the first episode may reveal a lot. First, the sleep: is it true or feigned? Dumézilians would relate this epic event to the myth of Viṣṇu Anantaśāyin, raising a number of other issues involving Kṛṣṇa-Viṣṇu. Of course, we can shunt back from myth to epic, and read a full awakenness in Kṛṣṇa's sleep. But as an epic detail linking to other epic details, this is going to be called sleep. Anyway, the *double entendre* need not be lost sight of. Next, Duryodhana's and Arjuna's entries and waiting for Kṛṣṇa to wake up, Duryodhana seated comfortably at Kṛṣṇa's head and Arjuna standing with folded hands at the feet. There is no problem with Duryodhana's and Arjuna's actions. That Duryodhana should enter first is perhaps not an accident but explained by his warmongering. And that Duryodhana should *sit* and sit at the *head* is also expected. Not only is he Kṛṣṇa's son's father-in-law but is absolutely sceptical of Kṛṣṇa's divinity (the *Pāṇḍavagītā's* famous *tvayā-Hṛṣikeśa* is post-dated and in all probability a rationalization). On the contrary, even though Arjuna is Kṛṣṇa's cousin and brother-in-law, he has had enough glimpses of Kṛṣṇa's superiority. Besides, Duryodhana has come as a king to another king, proud and confident, whereas Arjuna has come to the principal Pāṇḍava ally. In fact, the epic narrative reminds us that Kṛṣṇa had just returned to Dvārakā from Upaplavya after counselling the Pāṇḍavas on what to do in order to regain their rightful kingdom (was he giving them a chance to send his dear Arjuna to him knowing that Duryodhana himself might come on the Kaurava side?). The very configuration of Kṛṣṇa asleep and Duryodhana-Arjuna equipoised between his head and feet looks symbolic of the Kuru-Pāṇḍava situation with regard to him. He is supposed to be impartial to them; so, in the event of a war between them, a potential ally of both. Surely an ambiguity lurks here, for as the prime Pāṇḍava counsellor he is fully partial—in the Upaplavya council no less partial than Drupada or Virāṭa. It is interesting that at the end of that council he should suddenly announce his departure with Baladeva and other Vṛṣṇis and Andhakas. Does he not rush back, as it were, to lie down to his famous sleep so that Duryodhana-Arjuna should rush to him for martial help and sit-stand at his two ends? If my argument is on the right track, then there is no denying that Kṛṣṇa is abetting war. Through his spies Duryodhana should know when Kṛṣṇa is back at Dvārakā, and in the Upaplavya council Kṛṣṇa himself had endorsed Drupada's suggestion that the Pāṇḍavas should send for allies (the Yādavas being prime potential). Kṛṣṇa as counsellor and Kṛṣṇa as potential ally seem to be symptomatic of the ambiguity we are probing.

Anyway, the configuration of Kṛṣṇa asleep and Duryodhana-Arjuna at his two ends, seated-standing, reminds one of Oedipus' two sons, poised to be engaged in one of the most disastrous *Brudermords* of legend, oracle-driven, try one after the other for their father's blessings. Oedipus may be called truly impartial for he denies them both his blessings thus causing failure to both. Not only that, he also supplements it with a curse that they will both die at one another's hand. In the light of such impartiality, Kṛṣṇa's supposed impartiality is surely to be doubted. In other words, Kṛṣṇa has a motive; Oedipus is free of motive. He speaks and acts out of passion. Kṛṣṇa does not. But what is Kṛṣṇa's motive? If he is indirectly helping to cause war, as I seem to be indirectly arguing, then his motive may be Kuru-Pāṇḍava destruction, the role assigned to him, once again speaking retrospectively, according to the battlefield.

Sleep, Duryodhana-Arjuna, and now Kṛṣṇa wakes. Naturally he sees Arjuna first: but was it designed that he should see Arjuna first? He has to accept Duryodhana's priority by entry, and *dharma* there stipulates that he answer Duryodhana first (Drupada mentioned this aspect of kingly *dharma* in the Upaplavya council); but then he has seen Arjuna first. This creates a catch in *dharma* which he unlocks by the fact that Arjuna is younger. No precedence is provided for this particular priority of youth over age—he seems to be relying on Duryodhana's cavalier sense and sporting spirit. Then he offers his terms: he won't himself fight but be there. However, he has a famous army of ten million *gopas*, his equal in battle. Let them choose: Arjuna first. Baladeva, too, is going to announce that he won't fight in this war, but there is a difference between Kṛṣṇa not taking arms and Baladeva not. Baladeva's is pacifism; he will be away. But Kṛṣṇa will be a passive actor. Let us not raise the much debated question of the spirit of Kṛṣṇa's passivity, though we must recall once again that every single strategy in the war, except Bhīṣma's fall which Bhīṣma himself 'plans', is motivated by the unarmed charioteer of Arjuna. As to Arjuna picking him single and unarmed, against the invincible Nārāyaṇas is epic action with a mythic depth. Of course it has its epic background and links like the Subhadrāharaṇa and Khāṇḍavadāhana episodes; but it also relates to what Bhīṣma is going to tell us in the Kaurava council about Nara-Nārāyaṇa. Considering the simultaneous duality and unity of Nara and Nārāyaṇa at the mythic level, the epic pull for Arjuna to Kṛṣṇa is fully understandable. When Kṛṣṇa asks him later why he chose him against such seeming odds, Arjuna does not mouth routine humility, for he, too, is proud, no less perhaps than Duryodhana. He says that like Kṛṣṇa he also can kill all enemy single-handed; so it was not war as such that had motivated him his choice. His choice was motivated by his long-felt desire to have Kṛṣṇa as his charioteer in battle. As to Duryodhana, it is natural that he should be happy with his portion. Since he has had no occasion to believe in Kṛṣṇa's divinity, ten million Nārāyaṇas to him should be superior to Kṛṣṇa unarmed. With Bhīṣma, Droṇa and Karṇa, and with a great many allies, he feels confident of victory. Thus confidence is pitted against confidence, pride against pride, and the cousins go their several ways. Our first episode ends. A one-*adhyāya* episode, bare of details, it has a whole lot of meaning, a part of which I have tried to decipher, in terms of Kṛṣṇa's motivation. And I have a hunch that at this stage Kṛṣṇa wants war.

As opposed to the first, our second episode is long, elaborate, slow-moving, internarrational—sixty-seven *adhyāyas* (*Bhagavadyāṇaparvadhyāyas*) in the Poona edition, about one-third the size of Udyogaparvan. First, we have the rationale built up of the *yana*: Yudhiṣṭhira's desire for peace and appeal to Kṛṣṇa for final counsel, the other Pāṇḍavas' and Draupadī's opinions in favour of either peace or war, and Kṛṣṇa's decision to go on a final mission to the Kauravas. Then the journey, a few details. Next the narration shifts to the Kauravas preparing for Kṛṣṇa's arrival. They are divided: the elders would accord him his due, the youngsters who are in charge would greet him but not bow down to him. After this is the arrival and the necessary protocol as well as personal visits by Kṛṣṇa (there is a detailed Kṛṣṇa-Kuntī-saṁvāda here). As ambassador Kṛṣṇa refuses Duryodhana's hospitality and takes Vidura's. Now follows the performance of the peace mission which is endorsed by the sages present with internarrational example. But Dhṛtarāṣṭra expresses his inability to accept the mission because of his son's 'perversity' upon which Kṛṣṇa tries his eloquence with Duryodhana. Bhiṣma, Droṇa and Vidura join him; but Duryodhana is inflexible and at Kṛṣṇa's chiding stages a walk-out. Kṛṣṇa proposes to the Kaurava elders that for the sake of peace Duryodhana be restrained, bound up and be sent to the Pāṇḍavas. The elders try a last bid with Duryodhana through Gāndhārī at whose righteous words Duryodhana stages a walk-out again. Then with his associates he hatches a plot to arrest Kṛṣṇa. Getting scent of it, Sātyaki alerts Kṛṣṇa who then manifests his cosmic form which overwhelms everyone. And it is at that climactic moment that Kṛṣṇa walks out from the Kaurava court. In the last section of the episode, Kṛṣṇa apprises Kuntī of the failure of the peace mission, who, on her turn, sends a pro-war message to Yudhiṣṭhira highlighting the feelings of a kingdomless king's mother.

It is interesting that the failure of Kṛṣṇa's peace mission is fused with the glory of his theophany. What in epic should be a matter of sadness is fused with what in myth is the greatest effulgence. The result is bewildering. It is only later, after Kṛṣṇa's exit from the Kaurava court, that its wise elders wake up to the reality of what has transpired, but without shedding the fine excess of the theophany. That is, the touch of myth is retained in the immediate epic follow-up. Among the Pāṇḍavas too after Kṛṣṇa reports his failure to desist Duryodhana from war, there is not much sadness: they seem reconciled to what is to be done. The pace now is brisk. When Kṛṣṇa closes his report by saying to Yudhiṣṭhira that the Kauravas, death-bound and all about to be annihilated, will not give him his kingdom without war, Yudhiṣṭhira turns to his brothers and tells them to set up the army divisions. They realize that they have now hit war. What partly helps them realize is the concluding speech of Kṛṣṇa which opens with a deliberate exaggeration. He says in so many words how, upon the Kaurava elders' failure to dissuade Duryodhana from war, Duryodhana asked everyone to assemble at Kurukṣetra and how Bhīṣma had been appointed 'Marshal'—acts still to be done if we go by the narrative sequence. This surely is one of Kṛṣṇa's famous subterfuges, but what interests us is the motive behind it. If Kṛṣṇa had not wanted war, he would not have tried to egg them on. Also, Kṛṣṇa does not seem sad that war could not be averted. Imagine Yudhiṣṭhira in Kṛṣṇa's place: he should have been extremely sad. Of course, for Kṛṣṇa we can say that he is generally aware of the mythic dimensions of his epic role. Therefore, the last he should be is sad. Even in the Mausalaparvan, he does not show Yudhiṣṭhira's kind of sadness. However, it would be absurd to say that he is always functioning on the mythic level. But he shifts so quickly from the epic to the mythic and back to the epic again that it is impossible to bind him by either epic or mythic strands. In other words, ambiguity seems to come naturally to him. At the epic level, his peace mission is more protocol and intimidation than mission. He comes to sell peace, he goes back buying war, and without regret. A diplomat who is more interested in the politics of diplomacy than in the diplomatic text, he may remind us of Odysseus, but only up to a point. Epic Kṛṣṇa is more subtle and more glorious.

Mythic Kṛṣṇa's prime signifier here, the theophany in the Kaurava court, links up with the other and more important theophany (*Mahābhārata, Bhagavadgītā*). The cue for this theophany is Duryodhana's plot to arrest him, and thus deprive the Pāṇḍavas of their prime ally and counsellor. Kṛṣṇa has come with his kinsmen Sātyaki and Kṛtavarman, but Duryodhana hatches his plot considering him away from the Pāṇḍavas, Andhakas and Vṛṣṇis. For that reason, the theophany is primarily addressed to Duryodhana who must realize that Kṛṣṇa is never alone: he contains Pāṇḍavas, Andhakas, Vṛṣṇis in him; he contains more. As scholars have pointed out, this is a creation theophany: Kṛṣṇa creates the whole world out of his body. The full text (1b-11) in the Ganguli-Roy translation is here:

> Kesava, that slayer of hostile division, endured with great energy, addressed Dhritarashtra's son, Duryodhana, and said, "From delusion, O Suyodhana, thou regardest me to be alone, and it is for this, O thou of little understanding, that thou seekest to make a captive by vanquishing me by violence. Here, however, are all the Pāṇḍavas and all the Vrishnis and Andha-

kas. Here are all the Adityas, the Rudras, and the Vasus, with all the great Rishis." Saying this, Kesava, that slayer of hostile heroes burst into a loud laughter. And as the high-souled Sauri laughed, from his body, that resembled a blazing fire, issued myriads of gods, each of lightning effulgence, but not bigger than the thumb. And on his forehead appeared Brahma, and on his breast Rudra. And on his arms appeared the regents of the world, and from his mouth issued Agni, the Adityas, the Sadhyas, the Vasus, the Aswins, the Maruts with Indra and the Viswadevas. And myriads of Yakshas, and the Gandharvas, and Rakshasas also, of the same measure and form, issued thence. And from his arms issued Sankarshana and Dhananjaya. And Arjuna stood on his right, bow in hand, and Rama stood on his left, armed with the plough. And behind him stood Bhima, and Yudhisthira, and the two sons of Madri, and before him were all the Andhakas and the Vrishnis with Pradyumna and other chiefs bearing mighty weapons upraised. And on his diverse arms were seen the conch, the discus, the mace, the bow called *Saranga*, the plough, the javelin, the *Nandaka*, and every other weapon, all shining with effulgence, and upraised for striking. And from his eyes and nose and ears and every part of his body, issued sparks of fire mixed with smoke. And from the pores of his body issued sparks of fire like unto the rays of the sun.

This theophany to Duryodhana is the reverse of the theophany to come, the theophany to Arjuna, taking us back, can we say, to our first episode—Arjuna standing with folded hands at Kṛṣṇa's feet, the *bhakta*; and Duryodhana seated at his head, the defiant *abhakta*, so to speak. Destruction for Arjuna to show, speaking metaphysically, that there is no 'killing' in the ordinary sense; and creation for Duryodhana to show that, however much he may try, he can't destroy. Both visions are terrifying—maybe with a difference of magnitude—but because of its reception the one has come down to us as the height of metaphysics, while the other has remained primarily an epic event. Surely there is subsidiary reception by the elders, even Dhṛtarāṣṭra whose sight is temporarily restored by Kṛṣṇa's grace, and there is wonder and joy; but the chief receiver is merely intimidated. For the time being, for as on

Kṛṣṇa's glorious exit the elders urge him to make peace, he merely sulks. If the second theophany is to mythicize war, then the first theophany is to mythicize peace, thus taking away the distinction between the two. And if there is no distinction between war and peace, then, shunting back from the mythic to the epic, how can we say that Kṛṣṇa's mission was a peace mission? But ostensibly it was, and this takes us to our third episode, the Karṇa-Kṛṣṇa-saṁvāda, the first part of the Karṇanivāda (the second being the Karṇa-Kuntī-saṁvāda), four *adhyāyas*.

Of these four the first is devoted to Kṛṣṇa telling Karṇa of his birth and of the legitimacy of his Pāṇḍava status and then offering him the Pāṇḍava kingdom as the eldest brother. The second takes up Karṇa's *dharma* which impels him to decline Kṛṣṇa's offer on the grounds that raised by Adhiratha and Rādhā as a sūta he cannot now disown them as his parents; and that, since his benefactor and friend Duryodhana has ventured on this war relying on him, he cannot now ditch him. Then predicting Pāṇḍava victory he describes the impending war as a *yajña* in which the chief factor is Kṛṣṇa. In answer in the third *adhyāya*, Kṛṣṇa confirms that prediction. His description of the impending war is in terms of a *yugānta* in which the factors are the Pāṇḍavas and the refrain he uses, *na tadā bhavitā tretā na kṛtaṁ dvāparaṃ na ca*, has clear mythic implications. The fourth *adhyāya* is again given to Karṇa in which he cites various bad omens and nightmares signifying Kaurava destruction. His own dream he relates projecting the Pāṇḍavas clad in white and seated on white seats in a high and beautiful palace, while the earth is flooded with blood, and Yudhiṣṭhira perched on bones eating choice food from a golden platter and devouring the worlds—is charged with mythic significance. His other dreams, too, have a similar significance.

Now Karṇa's renunciation of a sure Pāṇḍava future and courting heroic death in a single combat with Arjuna may remind us of the second important moment in Achilles' career in the *Iliad*. Achilles has just received the shocking news of his friend Patroclus' death in battle with Hector. He groans and howls, but jumps into action. He has been idle too long, and it is because of his idleness that his friend had to fall. He will now go and avenge his friend's death on Hector. His mother Thetis rushes up from the deeps lamenting for her son, for she has knowledge for Zeus that Achilles' death will be imminent when he kills Hector. She tries to dissuade him by revealing that knowledge. But that cannot deter him. He must die one day, and he doesn't care whether it is today or tomorrow; but how can he *not* avenge his friend's death? His heroic *dharma* does not really leave him a choice. The event is pure epic, for, in spite of his nymph mother and her Olympian connection, he does not have recourse to myth. In fact, one may even say that he is acting epically against myth. Karṇa does not have Achilles' passion but all the determination that goes with *dharma*. Perhaps he is the most heroic figure of the *Mahābhārata*.

Karṇa may also in part remind us of Hagen in the latter *Aventeur* of the Middle High German epic *Nibelungenlied*. When an invitation came to King Gunther from Hungary, his lord counsellor Hagen advised him not to accept it, for he knew that Gunther's sister Kriemhild, now married to King Etzel, would by all means avenge her earlier husband Siegfried's death. The invitation was a cover. But Hagen was vetoed down. While at Danube looking for a boat, Hagen came across three nixies or water spirits who told him his future. Neither he, they said, nor any of his companions except the chaplain would cross back Danube. This was the only supernatural occasion in the poem, and Hagen tested its truth by throwing the chaplain overboard who against all odds swam back to shore. So Hagen now knows that he is going to his death. He does not counsel the king to turn around, but goes ahead with fortitude and heroism. In fact, the Hagen that is born out of this event is no longer the mere counsellor but full heroic.

Revenons à nos moutons. Is Kṛṣṇa's overture to Karṇa a peace overture? If Karṇa joins the Pāṇḍavas, there is every chance that Duryodhana may back out (after all, Karṇa is Duryodhana's principal prop) and Kurukṣetra may be saved. In that respect this is good diplomacy, and we must give epic Kṛṣṇa credit to beat some of the best diplomats and greatest political philosophers like Kauṭilya or Machiavelli. Not only do the Pāṇḍavas regain their kingdom but also the security that they will never be threatened in the future—a serious geopolitical consideration if we go along with Van Buitenen's analysis in the introduction to his unfinished translation. In a Bhīṣma verse play on Karṇa called *Pratham Partha*, written broadly along the lines of Rabindranath's 'Karṇa-Kuntī-Saṁvad', Buddhadeva Bose (author also of a fine book on *Mahābhārata* recently translated as *The Book of Yudhiṣṭhir*) plays up this aspect of Kṛṣṇa in his dialogue with Karṇa. Incidentally, it is a powerful play on the imminence of Kurukṣetra (as much as his other Kurukṣetra play, *Saṁkranti*, set towards the end of the war and dealing with the death of Duryodhana), but like his great predecessor Buddhadeva Bose has given Karṇa the final decisive role. Now that Kṛṣṇa's mission has failed and Duryodhana has announced that he won't yield even a needle-pick of earth without war, Karṇa alone can stem the bloodshed by coming over to the Pāṇḍava side. Buddhadeva Bose reverses the *Mahābhārata* order of Kṛṣṇa and Kuntī's overtures to Karṇa, and throws in an extra third; an overture from Draupadī (of course, Draupadī does not know that Karṇa is a Pāṇḍava by birth and so her husband; she only wants Karṇa to step aside, since he has nothing to gain from this war). But besides being a shrewd diplomat, Buddhadeva Bose's Kṛṣṇa is also the god he is supposed to be, and it is in that capacity that he reveals to Karṇa what he, Kṛṣṇa, will do in order to have Karṇa killed by Arjuna—the affair of the chariot wheel and the temporary amnesia on weapons. But all this, quite naturally for a modern writer, without the mythic dimension of Udyogaparvan.

Alf Hiltebeitel in a very readable and comprehensive book on Kṛṣṇa, *The Ritual of Battle: Krishna in the Mahābhārata* (Ithaca and London, Cornell University Press, 1976) has shown that all this is part of epic eschatology. He combines the methodologies of Dumézil and Biardeau, and reads not only a *yugānta* but also a *kalpānta*. But, I suspect, to quote myth as the prime rationale for epic is to make moral issues askew. And I wouldn't like to do that. I would rather stay with the ambiguity and read the epic again and again to decipher it. Does it matter if I stick to Giraudoux's *n'aura pas lieu* and not change to *aura lieu*? Even if I had called my paper by the other name, 'La Guerre de Kurukṣetra aura lieu', I would have ended up with the ambiguity. I have a feeling that ambiguity is one of the *Mahābhārata's* strong points. What I have called Kṛṣṇa's amphibiousness is Kṛṣṇa's strength. Let him be both god and man: the *Mahābhārata* is mine.

MARRIAGE AND FAMILY IN THE MAHĀBHĀRATA: SOME ASPECTS

S.G. KANTAWALA

INTRODUCTION

'THE *Mahābhārata* is not one poetic production at all, but rather a whole literature.'[1] It is a compendium of legends, narratives, didactic tracts, law, morality, philosophy, etc. In short, it is everything; it itself declares: 'What is in this work may be found elsewhere, but what is not in this work is to be found nowhere.'[2] And, in this brief poetic way it tells the story of its growth and development, as if of its becoming a literary cosmos.

The central narrative of the poem is the story of the two clashing families of cousins: Pāṇḍavas and Kauravas, their relatives, friends and allies. The history of the origin of these two families sheds some light on the social structure and practices, as well as the institution of marriage in the early period of ancient Indian history and culture.

The family is one of the important institutions of social organization, and a childless couple does not constitute even an elementary family.[3] Correlated with the institution of family is the institution of marriage. The principal purposes of marriage, according to the *Dharmaśāstra*, are: (1) *dharmasampatti*; (2) *prajā* and the consequent freedom from falling into hell; and (3) *rati* (sexual and other pleasures).[4] Every society has its own moral and ethical laws and considerations regarding family, pre-nuptial, nuptial and post-nuptial life, and society in general. The *Mahāhbārata* offers some glimpses into the societal and moral aspects. Moral laws change with the passage of time. The *Mahābhārata* is said to be a *kāvya* (1.1.73), a *dharmaśāstra* (cr. ed. 1.56.21) and an *itihāsa*

(1.56.21 = cr. ed. 1.56.19; *cf.* cr. ed. 1.1.17; 1.1.52; 1.56.18). In any case, it is a dynamic text. In what follows it is proposed to review from a dichronic point of view some episodes of family life and society in the context of the *dharmaśāstra* rules, especially the episode of *niyoga* in the context of Vicitravīrya's two widow-queens.

SYNOPSIS OF THE EPISODE

The Ādiparvan gives the genesis of the royal families of the Pāṇḍavas and Kauravas. Śāntanu could marry Satyavatī, the daughter of the fisherfolk-king, of whom he was enamoured. Devavrata (i.e. Bhīṣma) vouched for the abdication of his rightful claim to the royal throne and life-long celibacy (1.100.75ff = cr. ed. 1.94.40ff) for the sake of his father. Śāntanu had two sons: Citrāṅgada and Vicitravīrya from Satyavatī (also known as Matsyagandhā and Kālī; 1.101.2ff = cr. ed. 1.95.1ff). Citrāṅgada died in a battle (1.101.10 = cr. ed. 1.96.1), and Vicitravīrya died in his prime from tuberculosis (cr. ed. 1.96.51) leaving his two young beautiful wives, Ambikā and Ambālikā (1.102.65 = cr. ed. 1.96.52) childless (1.102.71ff = cr. ed. 1.96.51ff); and, consequently, he left no heir to the royal throne of Hastināpura, and this precipitated a crisis.

The queen-mother, Satyavatī called her stepson Devavrata, and asked him to marry and to procreate sons at her command (*niyogāt*) from the young and beautiful *putra-kāmā* widow-queens of her son Vicitravīrya for the continuance of the family; and to look after the kingdom by crowning himself (1.103.7ff = cr. ed. 1.97.7ff; cf. 1.104.38). He regretted that he could not accede to her request in view of his vow which was already known to her. He pointed out that what she was saying was bereft of *dharma* (*dharmād apetam* 1.103.23 = cr. ed. 1.97.23), and this led to the *dharma*-dilemma (cf. 1.103.24 = cr. ed. 1.97.24) for him.[5] Taking into consideration the problem of the continuance of the royal family and the observance of *dharma* and *satya*, he solved for himself the *dharma*-dilemma which he was facing at the request and command of the queen-mother by suggesting to her to invite a noble and virtuous Brāhmaṇa by payment of wealth (1.104.2 = cr. ed. 1.99.2). He styled this suggestion as *sanātanadharma* (1.103.25 = cr. ed. 1.97.25). On hearing this advice, she divulged to Devavrata that she had a son called Kṛṣṇa Dvaipāyana Vyāsa through the sage

Parāśara when she was a maiden as a result of a romantic meeting in the canoe by which he was crossing the river Yamunā; hence he was as much a brother from her (i.e. Satyavatī's) side, i.e. mother's side, as Devavrata was a brother from the father's (i.e. Śāntanu's) side, to Vicitravīrya. She sought Bhīṣma's permission to invite him.

Kṛṣṇa Dvaipāyana thereupon presented himself to her, and she commanded (*vacanāt niyogāt*; 1.104.36=cr. ed. 1.99.32) him to procreate sons for the continuance of the family. He agreed. He, however, suggested to his mother that the two-widow queens should observe a vow for one year. But she requested him to obey at once in view of the crisis. He then stated that, if Kausalyā (alias Ambikā) could bear his peculiar odour, form and body, she should approach him being pure after her menstrual period, well dressed and well ornamented (*vide* 1.104.47ff=cr. ed. 1.99.42ff). Accordingly, she got herself ready, but on seeing his untidy form and odourous body she closed her eyes; and the result of the union was the birth of the blind Dhṛtarāṣṭra (1.105.4-13=cr. ed. 1.100.4ff). Then Satyavatī spoke to her other daughter-in-law, Ambālikā, about the arrangement by *niyoga* of Kṛṣṇa Dvaipāyana Vyāsa with her with the same earlier procedure. She turned pale (*pāṇḍu*) when he approached her, and the result of the union was the birth of the anaemic Pāṇḍu whose sons were the renowned five Pāṇḍava princes (cr. ed. 1.100.14ff). Once again Satyavatī requested her son Kṛṣṇa Dvaipāyana to bestow one more son on the family, and solicited Ambikā at the time of her menstrual period for union with the same sage; but she did not honour the 'appointment' through fear,[6] and in her place she sent her maid who pleased the sage; and this union led to Vidura's birth (1.105.23ff=cr. ed. 1.100.27). Thus, three sons (i.e. 2+1) were born through the agency of Vyāsa.

DISCUSSION

The episode under discussion is a relic of the institution of *niyoga* (levirate system),[7] which came to be prohibited in later times with the changes in moral views governing the post-wedlock life. The ancient Indian law givers hold divergent views regarding the rules and procedures governing the operation of the *niyoga*-practice, and scholars are divided about its genesis.

It is significant to note that in this context the *Mahābhāratakāra* uses vocables, e.g. *viniyokṣyāmi* (1.103.7 = cr. ed. 1.97.7), *niyoga* (1.103.10 = cr. ed. 1.97.10), *niyuktaḥ* (1.105.4 = cr. ed. 1.100.4; 1.104.17 = cr. ed. 1.99.15), *nyayojayat* (1.105.22 = cr. ed. 1.100.22), derivable from *ni*+√*yuj*, 'appoint to, order, appoint anyone as',[8] with its derivative word *niyoga* meaning 'appointment of a wife or widow to procreate a son from intercourse with an appointed male'.[9]

It is significant to note that Devavrata was invited to marry the widows (*dārāś ca kuru dharmeṇa* ... /1.103.11 = cr. ed. 1.97.11) of his younger stepbrother. This suggests that in olden times the re-marriage of the widow/widows of the younger brother with the elder brother for the purpose of procreation of children was not considered obnoxious.[10] *En passant* it may be mentioned that the *Rāmāyaṇa* also provides an instance of the marriage of Bāli with Rumā, the wife of Sugrīva, the younger brother of Bāli, but it may be noted that this is an instance belonging to another culture.

Now, according to the *Manusmṛti* (9.57), the wife of a younger brother is to be looked upon as a daughter-in-law by a senior brother-in-law, and she is not to be approached. From this point of view, it is quite obvious that the *Dharmaśāstra* ruling would create a moral dilemma (*dharma*-dilemma) to Devavrata (*i.e.* Bhīṣma) in view of his vow of life-long celibacy and his abdication of his right to the royal throne, about which she knew, as it was done for her purpose. With a view to tiding over this dilemma, he suggested, while laying emphasis on *satya*, that she invite a virtuous Brāhmaṇa by offering wealth (*dhanena upanimantryatām*, 1.104.2 = cr. ed. 1.99.2). According to the *Gautamadharmasūtra* (18.4-8), 'a woman whose husband is dead and who desires offspring may secure a son from her brother-in-law' with the permission of the elders,[11] and, in addition to him, the other *Dharmaśāstra* texts add a *sapinda* and a *sagotra* of the husband.[12] The *Viṣṇudharmasūtra* (15.3) includes a Brāhmaṇa in the list of such appointees.[13] In the light of the directive in the *Viṣṇudharmasūtra*, Devavrata's suggestion to invite a virtuous Brāhmaṇa with the offering of wealth gains in significance. It tends to suggest the process of *dharmaśāstra-ization* at work. The remunerative aspect tends to suggest that it might have attracted some Brāhmaṇas to this obliging activity.

In the Pāṇḍu-Kuntī episode, a Brāhmaṇa endowed with *tapas* (cr. ed. 1.111.36) is suggested for 'appointment' (*niyoga*) by Pāṇḍu to Kuntī (1.121.7 = cr. ed. 1.113.30), even when she had expressed her unwillingness to agree to *niyoga*.[14] It is to be noted that in this episode the motifs of *vrata* and *tapas* are inserted. With reference to the members of the *brahmacārin* cult in ancient India, it is pointed out that 'as result of their severe penance they were endowed with special virile powers'.[15] In this light, the reference to the *vrata* and *tapas* gains in significance. Moreover, apart from its relationship with fertility, *tapas* was one of the factors of social vertical mobility in ancient India.[16]

Now, on Devavrata's declining the proposal of hers, the stepmother Satyavatī proposes to invite Vedavyāsa *alias* Kṛṣṇa Dvaipāyana, the senior stepbrother of the deceased king Vicitravīrya from the mother's side through Parāśara, when she was unmarried (1.104.7ff = cr. ed. 1.99.6ff). In this case, Vedavyāsa is a Brāhmaṇa as well as a senior brother-in-law, but it is obvious that the balance tilts on the latter relationship, and the influence of *dharmaśāstraization* here is also noticeable.[17] It is significant to note that Dvaipāyana is described as *devara* by Satyavatī (cr. ed. 1.100.2). It is interesting to note the semantic change coupled with a phonetic change in Gujarati of the vocable *devara*: Skt. *devara*, 'a husband's brother elder or younger'[18] Gujarati *diyara*, 'younger brother of a husband'.

The shock received by Vicitravīrya's widow-queens on meeting Vyāsa at the time of union and the trick of the deceitful substitution of the maidservant by Ambālikā tend to suggest that they either disapproved the appointee, or they disliked the practice; even though an attempt might have been made privately to explain the purpose and stores its importance (cf. cr. ed. 1.99.44-45). In this context, one may co-link the protesting arguments of Kuntī to Pāṇḍu, when the *niyoga* was suggested by him to her. It may be observed that all the necessary conditions to allow *niyoga* are not fulfilled in these cases.[19] It may be that this episode represents a stage prior to the codification of all rules. The episode under discussion tends to suggest that the custom of *niyoga* and widow remarriage might have existed side by side.[20]

The institution of *niyoga* seems to suggest that mating is not to be confounded with marriage customs. It revolves on the argument of the need to have a son for the continuance of the family, and it is to be noted that it involved extra-marital sex relations along with post-wedlock moral rules and values.

The two episodes point out that it was practised, in one case, when the husband died issueless; and, in another case, when the husband was impotent and the woman was in *ṛtu*. This reflects a stage of society, when sexual morals changed with the advancing control on the man-woman relationship from the stage of promiscuous sexual commerce in society in ancient days.[21] This evolution of moral and sexual ideas is seen reflected in the text when viewed in the light of the *Dharmaśāstra* teachings. The episode includes the period when a Brāhmaṇa came to be recommended indicating the process of *dharmaśāstra-ization* at work.

These episodes with the traces of the reflection of the changing moral ideas may also be connected with the Inversion-Theory (so called by Hopkins and originally propounded by Holtzman) regarding the *Mahābhārata*. According to this theory, 'the first poem was written for the glory of the Kurus and subsequently tampered with to magnify the Pāṇḍus.'[22] In the light of this theory, the episodes tend to suggest how some of the characters came to acquire favourable light with the process of *dharmaśāstra-ization*, even though these episodes continue to contain the earlier obnoxious relics. The diachronic levels preserved therein tend to reflect the changing and transforming morals of a society confronted with *dharma*-dilemmas.

NOTES

1. M. Winternitz, *A History of Indian Literature*, vol. i, Calcutta, 1927, p. 316.
2. V.S. Sukthankar, *On the Meaning of the Mahābhārata*, Bombay, 1957, p. 124; cf. *yad ihasti tad anyatra, yan nehasti na tat kvacit Mahābhārata* 62.53, (Gorakhpur Gita Press, with Hindi tr. vs. 2020)—*cr. ed.* 1.56.23.
3. See A.R. Radcliffe Brown, *Structure and Function in Primitive Society*, London, 1952, p. 51.
4. P.V. Kane, *History of Dharmaśāstra*, 2nd ed. vol. ii, pt. i, Pune, 1974, p. 429.

5. Yayāti faces a *dharma* dilemma in the Śarmiṣṭhā episode. See Bhakti Datta, *Sexual Ethics in the Mahābhārata in the Light of Dharmaśāstra Rulings*, London, 1979, p. 54.
6. Cf. *ny ayojayat* ϕ 1.105.22 = cr. ed. 1.100.22; *nākarod vacanaṁ devyā bhayāt*... 1.105.23—cr. ed. 1.100.22.
7. Cf. *levirate*<Latin *levir*, a husband's brother; akin, Greek *daer*. According to the ancient Jewish law, a childless widow married her husband's brother. See *New Webster's Dictionary of the English Language*, Delhi, 1979, p. 861.
8. A.A. Macdonell, *A Practical Sanskrit Dictionary*, Oxford University Press, 1954 p. 246.
9. P.V. Kane, *History of Dharmaśāstra*, 2nd. ed., vol. ii, pt.i , 1974, Pune, p. 599.
10. See Vālmīki, 'Kiṣkindhākāṇḍa', *Rāmāyaṇa* 6.23, 27; 8.21; 10.26 ff; 18.18 ff (Nirnay Sagar Press ed.); see cr. ed., Kiṣkindhākāṇḍa, pp. i, no. 5; 8.20; 10, 21 ff; 18.18 ff; 26.38.
11. P.V. Kane, *op. cit.*, p. 599.
12. P.V. Kane, *op. cit.*, p. 601.
13. See *Institutes of Viṣṇu* (*SBE*. vol. vii), pp. 61-62; according to J. Jolly, the *Viṣṇusmṛti*, *Vaiṣṇavadharmasūtra* and *Viṣṇudharmasūtra* are one (*ibid.*, Introduction, p. ix). See also P.V. Kane, *op. cit.*, p. 603. The *Viṣṇudharmasūtra* is assignable to A.D. 100 to A.D. 300, P.V. Kane, *op. cit.*, Chronological Table, p. xi.
14. The *Mahābhārata* 1.120.2 ff = cr. ed. 1.112.2 ff. For details, see S.G. Kantawala, 'Genetic Episode of Pāṇḍavas. Some Remarks', (paper read at the International Seminar on the *Mahābhārata*, Sahitya Akademi, New Delhi, 1987).
15. R.N. Dandekar, *Vedic Mythological Tracts*, Delhi, 1979, p. 208.
16. See S.G. Kantawala, *Cultural History from the Matsya-Purāṇa*, Baroda, 1964, pp. 45-46.
17. For Kumārila's remarks on Vyāsā's 'appointment', see *Tantravārtika*, p. 208 on Jaimini's *Sūtra* 1, 3, 7; P.V. Kane, *ibid.*, pp. 603-04.
18. V.S. Apte, *The Student's Sanskrit-English Dictionary*, Delhi, 1968, p. 260.
19. For conditions of *niyoga*, see P.V. Kane, *ibid.*, p. 601; S.G. Kantawala, *op.cit.*, pp. 79 ff.
20. See also P. Vora Dhairybala, *Evolution of Morals in the Epics: Mahābhārata and Rāmāyaṇa*, Bombay, 1959, p. 81; P.V. Kane, *ibid.*, pp. 555 ff.
21. The legend of Śvetaketu, the son of Uddālaka, depicts a period when women were free in ancient times, and he is accredited with stopping for the first time, all the free sex activities. See P.V. Kane, *ibid.*, p. 428; S.G. Kantawala, *op. cit.*, pp. 62 ff. D.R. Patil, *Cultural History from the Vāyu-Purāṇa*, Pune, 1946, pp. 44 ff, 156 ff; Bhakti Datta, *op. cit.* pp. 65 ff 108, 117.

As Śvetaketu is accredited with introducing controls on free sexual commerce, one may style this period after promulgation of the limitation as the 'Śvetaketu-period: Reformation', while the period prior to his promulgation of the limitation may be styled as 'Śvetaketu-period'.

22. V.S. Sukthankar, *op. cit.*, p. 14.

CONCEPTIONS OF DHARMA IN THE ŚRAMAṆICAL AND BRĀHMAṆICAL TRADITIONS: BUDDHISM AND THE MAHĀBHĀRATA

PETER DELLA SANTINA

INTRODUCTION

THIS paper is informed by the conviction that the evolution of Indian philosophy and religion can best be understood in terms of the interaction, and eventual synthesis of two ancient and originally quite distinct traditions. The traditions to which I refer are known as the Śramaṇical and Brāhmaṇical traditions respectively. The names of the traditions are, of course, derived from the key terms, 'Śramaṇa' and 'Brāhmaṇa' which refer, on the one hand, to the figure of the ascetic and, on the other, to that of the priest. Although the evidence from archaeological and literary sources may not be absolutely conclusive, there are certainly substantial grounds for supposing that the Śramaṇical tradition was originally associated with the pre-Aryan Indus valley civilization, and that the Brāhmaṇical tradition was originally the province of the Aryan migrants who came to India sometime later in the course of prehistory.

There exists sufficient information to establish beyond doubt the radical distinction between the religious culture of the Śramaṇical and Brāhmaṇical traditions. Indeed, the distinction has been taken note of by a number of modern scholars.[1] While the Śramaṇical tradition elevated liberation from the cycle of repeated birth and death to the level of the ultimate goal or highest good of conscious existence, the Brāhmaṇical tradition lauded longevity, prosperity, and progeny above all; and transcended the confines of the secular to the extent that it admitted the existence of a heaven modelled very much on a conception of a perfected version of this life. The Śramaṇical tradition developed the practises of asceticism and mental culture, that is, *yoga* or meditation, and evolved the conception of *karma* which was understood as the law of like causes and effects in the sphere of intentional action. The Brāhmaṇical tradition, on the other hand, emphasized the performance of social duty as determined by one's position within the caste structure. It accorded pride of place to the institution of the sacrifice or ritual action, as presided over by the priest or Brāhmaṇa, as the principal means of achieving the goals of conscious existence as they were conceived by the tradition. In general, Buddhism, Jainism, and Sāṅkhya-yoga may be regarded as the direct inheritors of the Śramaṇical tradition, while the Mimāṁsā, because of its conservatism, may be considered the prime example of a school directly descendant from the Brāhmaṇical tradition.

As it was suggested at the outset, the evolution of Indian philosophy and religion can best be understood in terms of the interaction and synthesis of the two ancient traditions which flourished on the Indian subcontinent. Indeed, synthesis began to take place very early in the course of their encounter. Both early Buddhism and the upaniṣads supply early and roughly contemporaneous instances of synthetic formulations of some of the principal concerns of the two traditions. Later, Sāṅkhya-yoga was incorporated virtually as a body into the ostensibly still orthodox Brāhmaṇical tradition. Still later, within the ostensibly orthodox tradition the advent of Advaitavedānta and post-classical popular Hinduism provided indubitable evidence of the synthetic and hybrid nature of the philosophical and religious tradition earlier and properly dubbed Brāhmaṇism. While the synthetic movement in Indian philosophy and religion affected not only the schools which continued to regard themselves as orthodox but also those like Buddhism which have always considered themselves separate and distinct, the nature of the synthesis evolved within the Buddhist tradition and within the Hindu tradition respectively were quite different.

The Buddhist tradition accorded the highest place within its religious and philosophical scheme to the Śramaṇical goal of liberation from the cycle of birth and death, emphasized the Śramaṇical practices of asceticism and mental culture, and retained the Śramaṇical conception of *karma*. It admitted the largely secular goals of the Brāhmaṇical tradition, i.e. longevity, prosperity, progeny, and heaven only provisionally. That is to say, the Buddhist tradition subordinated the religious and philosophical goals of the Brāhmaṇical tradition to those of the Śramaṇical. It never accepted at all the Brāhmaṇical conception of social duty as determined by one's position within the caste structure or the institution of sacrifice. Rather, the Buddhist tradition related the obtainment of the provisional goals of longevity and so forth, goals which had been final for the Brāhmaṇical tradition, to the efficacy of *karma* understood as the law of like causes and effects within the sphere of intentional action. In so far as positive causes are generated by intentional action, positive effects in the shape of happiness, prosperity and even heaven may be expected.

The Hindu tradition, on the other hand, particularly as it is exemplified by the synthetic and hybrid schools, admitted Śramaṇical goals, practices, and conceptions; but, in keeping with its original and fundamentally social orientation, only in a certain degree and in a particular context. The Advaitavedānta is perhaps alone in apparently subordinating the social and secular goals of the Brāhmaṇical tradition to the Śramaṇical goal of liberation. The religious and philosophical indebtedness of the Advaitavedānta to the Buddhist tradition is, in any case, well documented. Besides it may be hazarded that this very subordination of the secular goals of Brāhmaṇism to the transcendental goals of Śramaṇism on the part of the Advaita may be responsible for the elitism of the schools; and for the fact that, while it is universally praised as the apex of Hindu philosophy and religion, it is actually practised by only a relatively small number of Hindus. By and large, Śramaṇical elements within the popular Hindu synthesis are subordinated to Brāhmaṇical ones. A case in point is the Śramaṇical practice of asceticism. Although the practice was legitimized by texts such as the *Muṇḍaka Upaniṣad*, its acceptability within the Brāhmaṇical tradition was strictly circumscribed. The Śramaṇical practice of mental culture, on the other hand, was incorporated with less difficulty into the popular Hindu synthesis. This, of course, may be accounted for by the fact that mental culture is, in any case, instrumental to, rather than constitutive of the goals of conscious existence, and is clearly cappable of application not only to the transcendental but also to the secular goals of existence. The Śramaṇical conception of *karma*, which makes its first appearance within the Brāhmaṇical tradition in the upaniṣads, also came to be incorporated into the popular Hindu synthesis, the law of like causes and effects within the sphere of intention; however the tension between *karma* understood as at action and *karma* understood as ritual action, that is, sacrifice never wholly disappeared. Moreover, even in so far as the Śramaṇical conception of *karma* was admitted within the Hindu fold, it was subjected to certain modifications intended to render it compatible with the Hindu understanding of caste as it will be seen presently.

The *Gītā*, it is suggested, is an example *par excellence* of the popular Hindu synthesis of Śramaṇical and Brāhmaṇical elements. The opening dialogue between Kṛṣṇa and Arjuna contains a number of Śramaṇical elements as well as Brāhmaṇical ones. Nonetheless, the Śramaṇical content in the opening dialogue of the *Gītā* is clearly subordinated, and in one instance, which will be discussed in detail, manipulated by the Brāhmaṇical content. Therefore, I would suggest that the *Gītā* is typical of a popular Hindu synthesis in which Śramaṇical goals, practices and conceptions are definitely subordinated to the essentially social and secular concerns of the Brāhmaṇical tradition which retain their dominant and determining position. It may be further suggested that the *Gītā* is one of the earliest and as yet unsystematic attempts to accommodate, and, one might even say, to emasculate Śramaṇical religious culture, whose potency had been clearly demonstrated not only by its impact upon the Brāhmaṇical tradition but also by the immense popularity achieved by Buddhism during the millennia extending from the fifth century B.C. to the fifth century C.E.

CONCEPTIONS OF DHARMA

Let me now turn my attention to the conceptions of *dharma* entertained within the Śramaṇical and Brāhmaṇical traditions as they are represented in Buddhism, on the one hand, and in popular Hinduism in general and in the *Gītā* in particular, on the other hand. The term *dharma* has generally two meanings within the Buddhist tradition. The first is philosophical and even technical in character, and hardly concerns me in this paper. In the first instance, *dharma* means property, quality or factor of experience. In the second instance, the meaning of the term *dharma* is very ample indeed, almost all-encompassing in so far as the Buddhist universe of discourse is concerned. In this case, it refers to teaching of the Buddha and of the Buddhist tradition in general, that is, to the Buddhist way of achieving liberation. It could, therefore, be said that *dharma*, in this second and more important sense for my purposes, refers to Buddhist soteriology as a whole. This has prompted one contemporary scholar to suggest the term 'liberology' as a translation for the term *dharma* as it is understood within the Buddhist tradition, that is to say, the science of liberation. Formulated in this way, the definition of *dharma* clearly manifests the cardinal importance of the Śramaṇical goal of liberation.

However, the conception of *dharma*, as it is found within the Buddhist tradition because of its extremely wide signification, is not altogether without elements having reference to the provisional goals of happiness and prosperity in this life and in the next. Inasmuch as these essentially secular goals were primary for the Brāhmaṇical tradition, their appearance within the ambit of the conception of *dharma* within the Buddhist tradition where they have a provisional and prepadutic role may be interpreted as evidence of a degree of synthesism in the Buddhist camp. It should be pointed out, however, that the secular goals of happiness and prosperity in the Buddhist tradition are unequivocally subordinated to the transcendental goal of liberation. Moreover, in the Buddhist tradition, the secular goals of happiness and prosperity are secured not through ritual action as they were in the ancient Brāhmaṇical tradition, but rather by means of the efficacy of intentional action, *karma*, subjected to rational conceptions and moral principles.

Although the Buddhist conception of *dharma*, in so far as it is concerned with the securing of the secular goals of happiness and prosperity, is not altogether without reference to social contexts and structures, the social contexts and structures indicated are not those of caste but rather those of the family and the body politic. The best known example within the Buddhist tradition of injunctions having reference to specific social contexts and structures is perhaps found in the *Sigālovādasutta* of the Pāli canon. There the Buddha indicates particular roles and responsibilities to be fulfilled by individuals participating in the six social relationships: three familial, i.e. children, parents and spouses; and three extrafamilial, i.e. teachers, either spiritual or secular, and friends. Although there are also teachings of the Buddha intended to supply guidelines for the conduct of politics within the context of the nation state, nowhere have these injuctions reference to social position as determined by caste. Moreover, it is abundantly clear that such injuctions refer to the provisional and not to the final goal of conscious existence for the Buddhist tradition.

The distinction between provisional and final goals of conscious existence as conceived within the Buddhist tradition may perhaps loosely be correlated to the terms *dharma* and *abhidharma* respectively. The term *dharma*, as it has been shown, has an extremely wide signification within the Buddhist tradition. Qualified by the addition of the prefix *abhi* to form the compound *abhidharma*, it is traditionally understood to have reference specifically to the liberating philosophy of Buddhism in distinction to the term *dharma* in general which, as it has been explained, is not completely without social and secular application.

Within the Hindu tradition, on the other hand, the term *dharma* has been taken to mean duty, law, righteousness, moral merit, religious and social duties, or observances performed within the context of the social order as it is reflected in the caste structure. It is clear that the conception of *dharma* within the Hindu tradition has no direct reference whatsoever to the Śramaṇical goal of liberation which, by contrast within the Buddhist tradition, is the cardinal concept informing and determining the conception of *dharma*. That the conception of *dharma* within popular Hinduism is restricted to the social and secular sphere is also suggested by the enumeration of *dharma* as only one of the four goals of man or *puruṣārtha*. Liberation (*mokṣa*) is, of course, a separate goal.

Moreover, the Hindu tradition has developed and emphasized its own peculiar modification of the term *dharma* by the introduction of the prefix *sva* to form the compound *svadharma*. Translated by Deutsch[2] into 'own nature', the term *svadharma*, has no parallel to my knowledge within the Buddhist tradition. This is, of course, hardly surprising, because the term *svadharma* for popular Hinduism obviously refers to the social duties of the individual as they are determined by his position within the caste structure. On the other hand, caste, as it has been seen, has no place within the Buddhist tradition. The conception of *svadharma*, therefore, for popular Hinduism in general and for the *Gītā* in particular means the performance of the duties proper to one's position within the caste structure.

In adopting the translation 'own nature' for the term *svadharma* Deutsch admitted, perhaps ingenuously, the popular Hindu assumption that one's position within the caste structure is necessarily a reflection of one's moral and mental development, and, therefore, of one's nature. In this there is evident a conception of the working of *karma* understood, in this case, as intentional action, productive of moral and mental merit and demerit in which its efficacy is restricted apparently to the interface between this life and the next; in other words, to rebirth, or reincarnation. The Hindu conception of social order, as reflected in the caste structure, is impossible unless each life in itself is taken to be essentially static, frozen; a still-life photograph, albeit in a series of still-life each reflecting a birth in a particular social position. On the other hand, if *karma* is taken to be efficient, not only in the interface between one life and the next but rather within the context of a single life as well, functioning in the manner of an unbroken dynamic continuum in which death and rebirth are only particularly salient events, then the social order, as reflected in the caste structure, as an infallible indicators of the nature of one's duties, must inevitably break down. It may be suggested that the peculiar conception of the limited efficacy of *karma*, evolved within the Hindu tradition, represents an attempt to incorporate and subordinate the Śramaṇical conception of *karma* to the Brāhmaṇical conception of a stable social order reflected in the caste structure. The Buddhist conception of *karma*, on the other hand, conforms to the model of a dynamic continuum in which its efficacy is not restricted to the interface between one life and the next. It may be added that this conception of *karma*, conserved within the Buddhist tradition, is more faithful to the original Śramaṇical conception of *karma* freed from the Brāhmaṇical overlay of caste.

The Buddha, indeed, makes it clear in one of his earliest dialogues, which, according to tradition, occurred during the first few weeks after his enlightenment, that the individual's position within the social order or, to use Brāhmaṇical terminology, caste is determined not by the individual's birth but rather by his worth. That is to say, by the individual's moral and mental merit which is the sum total of the *karmic* potential he has amassed not only at the point of his precedent demise but rather at any given moment even within the context of a single life. Consequently, the conception of *svadharma*, as defined by one's position within the caste structure at birth accepted by popular Hinduism in general and by the *Gītā* in particular, is foreign to Buddhism, just because within the Buddhist tradition the duties proper to one's position within the social order may be altered at any moment by an alteration in the sum total of one's karmic worth affected by a single intentional act or by a series of intentional acts. Therefore, for the Buddhist tradition, one's position within the social order and consequently the duties proper to that position are not fixed at birth for the duration of a given life, but are part of a dynamic continuum capable of being altered at any time by means of efficient intentional action. It is, therefore, hardly surprising that the term and conception of *svadharma* has no obvious parallel in the Buddhist tradition.

Indeed, the Buddhists never had any great love for the conceptions of independent existence implicit in the prefix *sva*. Take, for example, the sustained Buddhist critique of the conception of independent existence *svabhāva*, a term which has also occasionally been rendered 'own nature' by translators. *Svabhāva*, however, has reference not, as in the case of the term *svadharma*, to a social phenomenon, but rather to an ontological or metaphysical entity.

GĪTĀ

Let me now turn my attention to the *Gītā* and, in particular, to the opening dialogue between Arjuna and Kṛṣṇa, which occupies the first and half of the second chapter. I am, for the purposes of this paper, excluding the second half of the second chapter, which in any case, contains only a workmanlike presentation of some meditative techniques bearing a close affinity with Sāṅkhya-Yoga practices.

Arjuna's complaint to Kṛṣṇa following upon his depression

contains a number of apparently Śramaṇical elements, particularly in the first portion of the speech. One might even be forgiven for thinking that Arjuna's protest is a genuinely Śramaṇical one. However, as it will be seen, Arjuna himself is confused about his motivations and his methods. And the dilemma from which he seeks refuge in a number of ill-defined Śramaṇical conceptions, is really a dilemma generated by a conflict between Brāhmaṇical social values. They are the values of the family, the kingdom, and the value of *svadharma* as determined by the caste structure.

Arjuna begins his complaint by declaring that he is filled with compassion (*kṛpā*).[3] Later, in the course of the second chapter, he confesses that he is affected by the defect of pity (*kārpaṇya-doṣa*).[4] Such admissions of the motivations of compassion and pity in other circles would be laudable. Compassion and pity are salient features of Mahāyāna Buddhist soteriology. Surprisingly, these conceptions never had much impact upon the Brāhmaṇical tradition, nor even upon the hybrid and synthetic schools which descended from that tradition. Their appearance here in the mouth of Arjuna is religious evidence of the post-Mahāyānic universe of discourse of the *Gītā*. Further substantial philosophical evidence of this will be offered later.

Arjuna's speech almost at once also betrays other concerns much closer to the Brāhmaṇical heart. It is clear that what is troubling Arjuna most is the fact that it is his own kinsmen, in other words, his own family members against whom he is called upon to fight. This concern, indeed, comes to the fore later in his speech when Arjuna makes more precise the actual nature of his dilemma. Before doing so, however, Arjuna voices another sentiment which is clearly Śramaṇical in tone. He says that there is no good in killing. He does not desire victory, kingdom or pleasure. Of what use are they?[5] Again, although these sentiments are apparently consonant with the values and attitudes of Śramaṇism it is soon made clear that Arjuna's concerns are not genuinely Śramaṇical ones. Indeed, the renunciation of kingdom and pleasure is avowed by Arjuna, only because he finds it more difficult to renounce the family or more precisely to effect the destruction of the family. As a matter of fact, Arjuna has clarified the real nature of his dilemma. The demands of the social order or more specifically the caste structure enjoin upon him a course of action which imperils the identity and existence of the family, an institution which in his eyes he is obligated to defend by virtue of an equally strong imperative. The conflict for Arjuna is between two Brāhmaṇical values: social order or castes structure, on the one hand, and loyalty to the family, on the other. The appearance of the apparently Śramaṇical declaration of renunciation seems hardly more than fortuitous, unless, of course, the real intention is the polemical dismissal of the Śramaṇical practice of renunciation by exposing its irrelevance.

Arjuna next goes on to deliver a long declamation clearly demonstrating his paramount concern for the preservation of the family as it was conceived within Brāhmaṇical circles. Not only is the declamation an expression of some of the principle concerns of orthodox Brāhmaṇism but it also contains a reference to a very ancient strata of religious beliefs and practices. Arjuna declares that the destruction of the family is criminal. The destruction of the family, he says, implies the annihilation of the family laws. From the latter follows the corruption of women, and the last and the worst the adulteration of castes. He who sets in motion such a disastrous chain of events must, indeed, be bound for hell, according to Arjuna. Moreover, the destruction of the family will mean that the ancestors are deprived of their customary offerings of food and the like. The author of such sins can only anticipate hell. Arjuna finishes this speech again with an apparently Śramaṇical flourish, declaring that it would be better if he were slain.[6]

Despite the apparently Śramaṇical conclusion, it is quite clear that Arjuna perceives in the path prescribed for him by his social duty within the caste structure a great evil, namely, the destruction of the family. The destruction of the family implies the destruction of the caste structure and the social order in general. It also implies the severance of the ritual continuity with the past represented by the institution of ancestor worship. The presence of this element in the *Gītā* indicates that the text contains some very old as well as some rather new ideas.

The thrust of Arjuna's argument, however, in the latter part of his speech is simply that the injuctions, imposed upon him by virtue of his position within the social order or the caste structure, i.e. to participate in the battle and to slay his kinsmen will bring about the destruction of the family and thus undermine the foundation of the caste strucuture and the social order in entirety. The crux of his dilemma, therefore, is that the injunctions of *svadharma* are in conflict with the imperative to preserve the family which, according to his conception, is the foundation of the social order itself. The injuctions of *svadharma*, therefore, appear to him to be self-destructive in character. Perhaps, the conflict evident here between the duty, enjoined by virtue of one's position within the caste structure, and the value of loyalty to the family or the clan betrays an historical crisis which took place at the point, when, having by and large subdued the non-Aryan opponents, the Aryans fell a pray to internecine strife.

In the opening passages of the second chapter, Kṛṣṇa commences his counselling of Arjuna with an open appeal to Brāhmaṇical values. He tells Arjuna that his attitude is unbecoming to an Aryan. The term Aryan was and is widely used in India, and it appears frequently even in Buddhist literature in such commonly known phrases as the Four Noble Truths and the Noble Eightfold Path. It is even applied to the class of persons who have transcended the limits of the mundane. There, however, it is shorn of its ethnic connotations and means simply noble or holy. The Buddhist redefinition of the term Aryan, originally undoubtedly an ethnic term denoting the migrant people who came to India from eastern Europe, is typical of a practice which extended even to the term *Brāhmaṇa.* The latter term, as it has been seen, was attached to someone within the Buddhist tradition according to his worth. There are, of course, also instances where the term *Brāhmaṇa* occurring in Buddhist literature retains its technical meaning, and denotes a member of the *Brāhmaṇa* caste. But such occurrences reflect merely the practical acceptance of the social reality as it existed.

In the mouth of Kṛṣṇa, however, the appeal to the conception of the conduct becoming to an Aryan appears unambiguously ethnic. It cannot refer to the concept of nobility and holiness as it existed in the Buddhist fold, but instead must refer to the conduct accepted as exemplary within the early Aryan society and the orthodox Brāhmaṇical tradition. This is made quite clear by Kṛṣṇa when he adds the warning that conduct unbecoming to an Aryan does not lead to heaven.[7] This clearly links the conduct of an Aryan, according to Kṛṣṇa's understanding, to the achievement of the highest secular goal of ancient Brāhmaṇism. The term in the Buddhist context, as it has been shown, specifically indicates a transcendental state, or pedagogical schemes leading to such a state and not heaven.

At this point, Arjuna gives voice to another sentiment which is so Śramaṇical that in the context it is almost startling. He says that it would be better to live by begging; and here he repeats his avowed affectation by the defect of pity and admits his confusion about his *dharma*,[8] thus offering an opportunity to Kṛṣṇa to shift the level of the discourse.

Kṛṣṇa promptly obliges. He introduces the shift in the level of discourse by drawing a distinction between the wise and the unwise. 'You may grieve', he tells Arjuna, 'but wisemen do not mourn for the living or for the dead.'[9] Kṛṣṇa then launches upon an exposition of the doctrine of non-origination (*ajātivāda*) which would not be out of place in the mouth of Gauḍapāda or for that matter in that of Nāgārjuna. While the style and content of the exposition closely resembles that of the great Buddhist philosopher of the first and second century C.E., the referent of the dialectical exercise is substantialized and ontologized in a form which is apparently none other than that of the supreme self or *paramātman*. That there has been more an adoption of pedagogical technique and less of philosophical insight is made clear at the outset. It, the supreme self, existed before and will exist afterwards, says Kṛṣṇa. It has nothing to do with incarnation in the living body. The objects of the senses like pleasure and pain are impermanent, and do not affect the supreme self.

Kṛṣṇa then declares, in a strikingly Nāgārjunian utterance, that there is no coming into existence of the non-existent, nor can there be any ceasing to exist of the existent. The truth about both of these, he says, is seen by the seers of truth. One might well compare this passage with a number from the *Mūlamādhyamakakārikā*, *Śūnyatāsaptati* and *Yuktiṣaṣtikā* of Nāgārjuna.[10] Therein Nāgārjuna declares that there is no origination either of the existent or of the non-existent. Nor again can the existent or the non-existent cease to exist. The perception of the existent and non-existent as interdependent and relative and their transcendence approaches the quintessence of the liberating philosophy of Buddhism.

But, immediately following upon this declaration, Kṛṣṇa hastens to clarify that the reality of which he speaks is none other than all-pervasive, indestructible, immutable being.[11] While Nāgārjuna steadfastly refuses to ontologize even emptiness (*śūnyatā*), Kṛṣṇa pronounces the transcendental reality beyond origination and destruction to be the eternal self. Having established the transcendentality of the supreme self by dialectically demonstrating its non-origination and non-destruction, Kṛṣṇa derives certain particular consequences for the sphere of action. The supreme self, he declares, is neither an agent nor an object. Those who imagine it to be an agent or an object are ignorant.[12] Nāgārjuna, of course, also demonstrated the emptiness of the conceptions of agent and object on the grounds of their interdependence. His purpose, however, was not to endow a supreme entity with immutable being. The consequence of the shift in the level of discourse introduced by Kṛṣṇa is that the individual is invited to quit the ranks of the unwise and join the ranks of the wise. The latter, who are privileged to knowledge of the eternal self, can neither kill nor be killed. Through knowledge of the eternal self, in other words, the knowing subject is supposed to acquire the characteristics of this all-pervasive, indestructible and immutable entity which, as Kṛṣṇa reiterates, weapons cannot cut and the like.[13] The practical consequence of the shift in the level of discourse, however, is that the agent is freed from any inhibition to act in a particular way, because action as such for the wise man is inconsequential in so far as he is privy to knowledge of and identification with the supreme self.

Next Kṛṣṇa again shifts the level of discourse subtly in a cleaver polemical manoeuver, also reminiscent of Nāgārjuna's dialectics in intention if not in acumen. In particular, Nāgārjuna's famous dilemmas which take the form 'if *A*, then not *B*, if not *A*, then not *B*' are called to mind. (Even if the self is impermanent, says Kṛṣṇa, evidently drawing upon an earlier strata of Buddhist teaching, subject to constant birth and death, then to inasmuch as birth, death and rebirth follow one another naturally and inevitably no particular onus need be attached to the agent who participates in this natural process.[14] It may be noted that in all of this no mention whatsoever is made of the Śramaṇical conception of intentional action as the final arbiter within the mundane or secular sphere. In other words, there is no evidence of any parallels of the Śramaṇical view present also in Buddhism, according to which the obtainment of the goals of happiness and prosperity is determined by the efficacy of intentional action guided by the moral principle of non-injury. The knowledge of the supreme self, in short, effectively frees the agent of any moral scruples.

Kṛṣṇa now takes up the orthodox Brāhmaṇical theme again by introducing the conception of *svadharma*. There is no greater good, he says, for a Kṣatriya than a battle required by duty. Such an opportunity, he declares, opens the door to heaven. The only alternative to following the path enjoined on him by his duty within the caste structure, suggests Kṛṣṇa, is sin and dishonour. On the other hand, he assures Arjuna the reward for fulfilling his duty is indubitable. If he prevails in the battle, he will win mastery over the earth, while, if he should be killed, he will win heaven.[15]

The Śramaṇical sentiments expressed in Arjuna's speech are largely ill-defined. They are presented out of context, and, in any case, their presence seems to serve merely as a fail for Kṛṣṇa's polemic in support of the conception of *svadharma*. In Kṛṣṇa's speech, on the other hand, the introduction of Śramaṇical, not to speak of Buddhist, conceptions is carefully calculated. Moreover, the transcendental critique of origination and destruction is expressed with a degree of precision, and there is even the suggestion of mimicking of a certain logical or dialectical technique, even if the obvious and immediate object of the exercise is to establish that the transcendentality of the supreme self is distinctly non-Buddhist. It is suggested that Kṛṣṇa's deliberate adoption of Buddhist material for a specific and, in fact, Brāhmaṇical end is crystal clear in Kṛṣṇa's speech. But what is the actual object of this skilful polemical manoeuver on the part of Kṛṣṇa? The demonstration of the transcendentality of the supreme self is intended to free Arjuna not *from* the performance of his social duty as determined by his position within the caste structure, but rather *to* perform his social duty as determined by his position within that structure. It is also intended to free him to perform his social duty as determined by his position within the caste structure without regard or responsibility for the apparently destructive nature of that duty. It is clear, therefore, that the performance of *svadharma* emerges as the supreme value in Kṛṣṇa's declamation. The demonstration of the transcendentality of the supreme self by means of the adoption of the transcendental critique of origination serves only to vindicate in a somewhat novel way the paramount position of *svadharma*.

This is not to say that there is no suggestion in Kṛṣṇa's words of a conception of liberation attainable through knowledge of and identification with the supreme self. Certainly, such a conception is at least implicit in other passages of the *Gītā*. Nonetheless, in the opening dialogue with Arjuna, it is not the liberating consequences of such knowledge and identification that Kṛṣṇa stresses, unless it is meant to be liberating only in so far as it enables Arjuna to perform his caste-determined social duty free from grief. The performance of such caste-determined social duty is, in any case, absolutely obligatory for the wise and the unwise alike.

Towards the conclusion of his speech, Kṛṣṇa returns with force to the traditional and largely secular goals of the Brāhmaṇical tradition, that is to say, dominion on earth or domicile in heaven. These essentially secular goals, which were provisional for the Buddhist tradition, are secured for Kṛṣṇa by the performance of *svadharma*. Kṛṣṇa's understanding of action (*karma*), therefore, approaches the earlier conception of ritual action in so far as action is ritualized for him by its conformity to the injunctions proper to one's position within the social order. It is this kind of action in conformity with one's position within the social order that ensures the obtainment of the secular goals of happiness and prosperity in this life and beyond. As far as any conception of liberation is concerned, that may be supplied through knowledge of and identification with the supreme or transcendental self. Again, it is worth pointing out that in all of this there is no obvious presence of the Śramaṇical conception of *karma* understood as intentional action productive of like effects. There is also no conception of a rational morality correlated to *karma* and evolved on the basis of principles such as reciprocity and non-injury.

Within the Buddhist camp the situation is quite different. There the institution of ritual action or sacrifice, so crucial for early Brāhmaṇism, is wholly absent. Nor is there any conception of social duty infallibly determined by one's position within the social order or caste structure. The provisional and secular goals of happiness and prosperity in this life and beyond are obtained by means of the efficacy of intentional action conditioned by the recognition of the principle of reciprocity and guided by the principle of non-injury. The principle of non-injury is, of course, also applied to specific situations and formulated in the shape of moral codes. The efficacy of intentional action, in so far as it is governed by the principle of non-injury and guided by the appropriate moral codes, ensures the obtainment of the provisional goals accepted by the tradition. The obtainment of the secular goals of happiness and prosperity in this life and beyond is, therefore, the product of intentional action operating in accord with principles of rational morality. Moreover, the governance of intentional action in accord with the principles of rational morality for the Buddhist tradition is encouraged not by the dictates of a particular conception of the social order, but rather by what one might term an universal imperative of conscious existence, that is, the desire for happiness and prosperity. In so far as the supramundane or transcendental sphere is concerned, in other words, the ultimate goal of the Buddhist tradition, it is liberation that is secured by the dissolution of duality or polarity as exemplified by the conceptions of existence, non-existence origination, destruction, agent, object and the rest.

In Kṛṣṇa's address to Arjuna, it was seen that the introduction of the transcendental critique of origination and destruction, agent and object did not free the individual from his social duties as determined by his position within the caste structure, but rather freed him to perform them without inhibition. In the Buddhist context, the transcendental critique of existence, non-existence, origination, and destruction, agent and object also does not absolve one of the obligation to conform to the principles and codes of rational morality. Nonetheless, two points ought to be stressed in this connection. First, within the Buddhist tradition, although the principles of morality may remain constant, the formal moral codes which they inspire are always subject to modification in relation to particular circumstances that may be encountered in the course of their application in practice. Secondly, in so far as the dissolution of duality or polarity entails the abandonment of egocentrism, it automatically, as it were, removes the possibility of action being motivated in a manner contrary to the principle of non-injury.

CONCLUSION

What then of the moral message of the *Gītā* as it is found in the opening dialogue between Kṛṣṇa and Arjuna? On examination, it appears to be simple enough. Perform one's social duty, *svadharma,* as it is determined by one's position within the caste structure, and one will be rewarded with dominion on earth and domicile in heaven. This is an unambiguously Brāhmaṇical pronouncement. It takes particular care to safeguard the stability of the social order as it was conceived by early Brāhmaṇism, and it offers in return the obtainment of the secular goals of the tradition. The transcendental critique of origination and destruction, which serves to demonstrate the transcendentality of the supreme self, is introduced largely as a palliative for any emotional misgivings that may occur in the course of the performance of one's social duty, and also as a convenient device by means of which an apparent conflict between Brāhmaṇical values may be resolved. There is an ulterior suggestion of a kind of liberation to be had by means of knowledge of and identification with the supreme self, and freedom from emotional agitation by means of the application of a number of meditative techniques whose purpose is to achieve detachment from the objects of the senses.

However, is the primary moral message of the *Gītā,* as it is found in the opening dialogue, representative of a conception of morality which has evolved beyond an essentially primitive and ethnocentric standpoint and which is capable of universal application? It has been suggested that the primitive conception of morality, which existed in various cultural contexts during the pre-dawn of history, were in general ethnocentric and devoid of rational principles of morality which could be universalized. It would seem that moral conceptions in pre-Confucian China as they appear in the *Book of Odes* and other primitive literature conform to this picture. The situation could not have been very different among the ancient Greeks. This much is indicated by Plato's experimentation with various formulations of a principle of rational morality capable of universal application. Plato's development of the principle of enlightened self-interest, which has much in common with the principles of reciprocity and non-injury evolved in the Buddhist and Confucian traditions, was clearly considered by him as an advance over other ethnocentric and irrational moral formulae that were incapable of universal application.

In India too, ancient Brāhmaṇical literature as exemplified by the Vedas, Brāhmaṇas and other pre-Upaniṣadic texts provide no clear formulation or presentation of fundamental principles of rational morality capable of universal application. It appears evident that the opening dialogue of the *Gītā* is extremely hybrid and synthetic in nature. It contains material clearly informed by rather late developments within the Śramaṇical and Buddhist traditions. The references to compassion and pity, and still more so to the sophisticated transcendental critique of origination and destruction would seem to suggest a post-Mahāyānic universe of discourse. On the other hand, the references to the practice of ancestor worship would seem to reflect primeval religious practices. It has been suggested that the Śramaṇical and Buddhist elements in the opening dialogue of the *Gītā* are introduced largely for polemical and pedagogical motives. The central conception of the text would appear to be patently Brāhmaṇical. Therefore, the moral message of the *Gītā*, in so far as I can determine, conforms to the primitive and ethnocentric conceptions of morality common to ancient Brāhmaṇism. The level of evolution of the morality portrayed is one in which rational principles capable of universal application have not yet been identified and systematically applied. But it is perhaps a mistake to look for rational and universal principles of morality in an epic text. For is not the epic, by its very nature, representative of that strata of cultural consciousness which belongs to the pre-dawn of rational, universal and systematic conceptions of the nature and goals of conscious existence? The opening dialogue of the *Gītā*, notwithstanding the presence of some rather sophisticated psychological and philosophical ideas, does not stray materially from the epic vision, and the morality reflected therein may be said to be amoral in so far as rational and universal principles of morality are not to be found there. Perhaps, one might do better to look for such moral conceptions elsewhere.

NOTES

1. G.C. Pandey in his *Studies in the Origins of Buddhism,* Delhi, Motilal Banarsidass, 1974 and L.M. Joshi in *Brahmanism, Buddhism and Hinduism* (Kandy, 1973) have discussed the nature of Brāhmaṇical and Śramaṇical religious culture.
2. E. Deutsch, *The Bhagvad Gītā,* Canada, Holt, Rinehart and Winston, 1957, p. 8.
3. E. Deutsch and S. Radhakrishnan, *The Bhagavadgītā,* London, 1960, George Allen & Unwin, agree in general in their respective translations of the term *kṛpā.* See their translations of the *Bhagvadgīta,* I. 18.
4. *Bhagvadgītā* ii. 7.
5. *Ibid.,* i, 32 ff.
6. *Ibid.,* i. 38-46.
7. *Ibid.,* ii. 2.
8. *Ibid.,* ii. 5.
9. *Ibid.,* ii. 11.
10. *Ibid.,* ii. 16. Compare this passage with *Mūlamādhyamakakārikā,* xiii, 8-11 and xv 5-7; *Śūnyatāsaptati* and *Vṛtti* 4 and *Yuktiṣaṣtikā* 1-11 of Nāgārjuna.
11. *Bhagavadgītā* ii. 17.
12. *Ibid.,* ii. 19.
13. *Ibid.,* ii. 23.
14. *Ibid.,* ii. 26.
15. *Ibid.,* ii. 37.

REFLECTIONS ON THE CONCEPT OF ACTION IN THE GĪTĀ

S. PAUL KASHAP

I MUST begin with an admission that I am not a Sanskrit scholar, nor am I an expert in the historical intricacies of Indian systems of thought. I have been studying philosophy for the past thirty-five years, and my chief interest has been in Western philosophy. However, I have for all those years been studying the texts of the Upaniṣads, the *Bhagvadgītā* and the *Brahmasūtras*; and trying with varying degrees of frustration and annoyance to get a clearer grasp of the strictly philosophical content of these texts. For I find that, although where the philosophically significant passages are concerned the writers of these texts do *mean* what they say, they are confoundingly reluctant to *say* what they mean. There is an Alice in Wonderland quality about their utterances. They have an incurable tendency to speak in aphorisms. Nothing is straightforward, except in places where what is said is so commonplace that one wonders why it needed to be said at all. For a person, who is philosophically oriented, they create an impression of mystery and ineffability.

I do not mean to imply that Indian philosophical literature as a whole has a similar character. Here I agree, of course, with Professor Matilal's assessment and his quite valid observation that a look at the *Nyāya-Vaiśeṣika*, for instance, makes it clear that 'the business of most classical philosophers of India was solid and down-to-earth philosophic argumentation, and not the creation of mystical illusion or poetic description of mystical experiences'.[1] But the term 'most' does not cover 'all', and does leave out some, especially the metaphysically significant ones, when one is not speaking about the 'systems' but about the *Upaniṣads* and the *Bhagvad-*

gītā. The mystery is generated by the evident incomprehensibility or at least by the enormous difficulty in comprehension of the philosophical content of some of the utterances of the Upaniṣadic sages. But there is nothing mysterious about the obvious fact that they are confoundingly difficult to break down into an intelligible form that would render them accessible not to everyone but even to that small percentage of the human race, who have dedicated their lives and their intelligence to understanding and articulating the intentional content of their utterances. For that is the whole point of philosophic understanding, viz. to reconstruct and bring to light the complexities of their thought and reasoning which we find in the texts of the *Upaniṣads* and the *Gītā*.

It is a well-recognized fact that, while the *Gītā* may well have been *compiled* by one individual, the ideas, views and theories, right or wrong, that find expression in it are not the ideas, views and theories attributable to any *one* but to *several* different individuals, spread over a period of hundreds, if not a couple of thousands of years. Furthermore, the mode, the manner and the linguistic style in which these individuals expressed themselves is that of *poetic* geniuses rather than that of philosophers. They were metaphysical poets of the highest order. They gave expression to their responses, often extremely sensitive and insightful responses, to a variety of situations and contexts which they found that they themselves and other human beings faced. But just as it makes very little sense to ask, in respect of lines of poetry, whether what a poet utters or writes as a poem is true or false, similarly it makes very little sense to ask whether what the poetic sages of the *Gītā* said, taken literally, and as they said it, is true or false. When, for instance, we hear or read a poet saying 'April is the cruelest month, breeding lilacs out of the dead land, mixing/memory and desire, stirring/dull roots with spring rain', we may lose ourselves in the imagery and in the memories recalled, or the feelings and emotions, pleasurable or painful, that are evoked. We may be attracted to them or repelled by them, or we may not be moved by them in any way whatsoever; but it is perfectly senseless to ask whether what is said, in these lines, is true or false. I do not mean to imply that one cannot, nor is it logically impossible for one to, respond to these lines by uttering aloud or to oneself 'Yes, I agree', meaning that one understands and empathizes with what the poet wants to convey, and appreciates how beautifully he has expressed it. But this is not an agreement to its truth or falsity, but an agreement about the similarity of one's own sentiments with those of the poet, or of the poet's with our own.

The utterances of the *Gītā's* sages are full of metaphors, similes and allegories. That is the way it should be, for they are poets *par excellence*. They display incredibly fertile imaginations, and superb heights of metaphysical speculation. And to appreciate their utterances properly is to accept them and take them to be exactly what they are, and not to be misled into taking them as statements that can be scrutinized as to their truth or falsity.

There is one other point which is in order in this context. The philosophical *validity* of a statement does not rest, nor can it be established, on the grounds of its being consistent with what was historically believed about (or associated with) the statement. The fact that people have the kind of reason they have for believing a statement to be true does not mean that the statement cannot be false. For they may take the statement to be true on grounds which they believe to be adequate and appropriate without yet being aware that those kinds of grounds have no logical connection with the truth of the statement. So that if the statement were believed to be true on those kinds of grounds, then it would be an instance of false belief. A statement, expressing a belief, is true when it involves the use of a sentence to make an assertion on grounds that are valid, in the sense that they are logically related to the kind of facts the assertion is about. A philosopher or a person with philosophical insight may make a statement on having clearly perceived and grasped the logical grounds for its truth, though these may not be generally believed, at a given historical juncture, to be connected with its truth, and he may use a sentence to express his belief in the form of a statement that is true on grounds, which, in fact, are the only grounds it could have for it to be true.

It is philosophical insight, I think, rather than historical scholarship that is required to grasp the truth of a statement of philosophical import made at whatever point in history. What that statement was supposed to be saying, i.e. its assertive content, can be understood only by articulating what the logical grounds of its truth were and by showing that, in fact, these were the grounds that the philosopher *did have* for making the statement.

To unearth these grounds and to express them in a language that the original writer himself might have used, if he were requir-ed to make himself intelligible in the contemporary terminology of any given age, is, in one significant sense, to engage in philoso-phical interpretation. It has very little, if anything, to do with the history of the use of a sentence or an expression. When people do engage in unearthing the history and record of the use of a sen-tence or expression, they offer, at best, a historical interpretation as distinct from a philosophical one.

It is very easy to make the mistake of taking historical inter-pretation to be the same as philosophical interpretation, and we need to be on guard. All the commentaries that I have come across involve this confusion, and hence fall short, in varying degree, of making the philosophical content of the most significant passages in the text accessible and intelligible. None of them succeeds in offering any illumination about any of the central notions in the text, such as action (*karma*), knowledge (*jñāna*), ignorance (*ajñāna*), self-knowledge (*atmajñāna*), desire (*kāma*), attachment and non-attachment.

The commentators almost invariably concentrate on 'God' or the 'absolute'. It is a colossal puzzle to try to explain how the no-tion of Brahma or God got introduced into the attempts to make the *Gītā* intelligible. How did *Brahmajñāna* get rendered into 'knowledge *of* Brahma' and *atmajñāna* into 'knowledge *of* the self'? Poets do have a licence to personify and make into substan-tives anything they please; but surely one cannot begin to take them literally. Of course, there are hints in the texts of the *Upani-ṣads* and the *Gītā* about the nature of the ultimate source of the phenomenal world that is linked in a causal chain of interdepend-ence, and a suggestion that the source or origin of this chain can-not itself be a link in that chain; that it itself cannot depend (for its being what it is) on anything other than its own nature, while everything else must ultimately be logically dependent on this source's being what it is. This is not metaphysical speculation but an insight into a logically necessary truth that the source of crea-tion cannot be of the same *logical type* as that which follows from it or which presupposes it. But the source is not something that you can say anything about that would count as a description. All one can say is *that* it must be, but not *what* it must be. It is *indes-*

cribable. Hence anything that can be described or identified is not *It*. To have understood this is to have understood the absurdity and futility of a search for the source, or an attempt to identify it with a substantive entity in any form.

It is quite obvious that the question that the sages grapple with in the *Gītā* is not a trivial question. The question is: 'How should one live?' It is the same question that was posed by Socrates. It is concerned with human life, with the human predicament. The sages assume that a particular *kind* of thinking is necessary in order to have a reasonable hope of grasping the correct answer to it. They also assume and, to their credit, recognize, that this is an extremely general question. There are several different ways, they suggest, in which this question could be construed; depending on the context in which it is asked, and on the particular individual who is asking it, who is seen as a member of a small or a large group or set of individuals, distinguished in terms of certain mental and physical predicates. They are suggesting that there is no *one* answer that would count as an answer to the question for every individual or in any and every circumstance. The variation in the necessary and sufficient conditions making an individual situation in which it is appropriate to ask this question are too complex and various for anyone to take full account of them and to arrive at a foolproof answer in any given case.

There are great difficulties involved in understanding the nature of the question itself, and the sages were very aware of these difficulties. For one thing, any given instance of an action that one performs is not an isolated piece of behaviour or activity, but is, in a very significant sense, a part of one's life. It is a part of one's life in the sense that it is necessarily connected with a host of factors, for instance, one's genetic structure, one's dispositions, the ideas one entertains about oneself and the world, and one's beliefs about appropriate or inappropriate responses to the situations one encounters in living in the world as a member of a social group whose identity is more or less specifiable by reference to a particular set of predicates that are truly applicable to it. By 'truly applicable' is meant that a given member of one group can be distinguished from a member of another group in as far as certain specific physiological, psychological and/or social characteristics that are predicable of an individual are descriptively applicable to a member of that group as distinct from another group. The conceptual scheme that the *Gītā* sages employ for this purpose is similar in *function* (but not similar in *goal*) to the conceptual scheme used, for instance, by Freud in introducing the notions of the 'conscious', 'preconscious' and 'unconscious' and the 'ego', 'Id' and 'superego', to facilitate giving a reasonable explanation of certain kinds of phenomena which are found puzzling with regard to human beings, and about which we raise certain questions with a view to seeking a plausible answer.

Now the concept of *guṇas* is offered in the context of Indian thought as one such, and perhaps the most important, conceptual scheme in terms of which the reasons for differences and similarities between individuals or things belonging to a given class or species, or between different species falling under the same or different general category, can be given a plausible explanation. The scheme serves, in fact, as the principle of individuation. Just as in the Freudian conceptual scheme the terms do not function as names of any substantive entities, similarly in the Indian conceptual scheme the terms for the *guṇas* (namely, *sattva*, *rajas* and *tamas*) are not be taken as names of any substantive entities. And one cannot but marvel at the extraordinary ingenuity of the ancient Indian sages in inventing the conceptual scheme of the *guṇas* that *does* aid in the understanding of individual differences. In fact, it would not be too far-fetched to suggest that the theory of the *guṇas* provides a far superior metaphysical foundation for the principle of identity of indiscernibles than does, for instance, the Leibnizean theory of monads.

There is one other question that needs to be considered about the nature of the utterances of the sages, namely, what *kind* of utterances are they? Granted that, in issuing these utterances in response to questions that were raised, the sages were performing 'speech acts'; but, apart from that, is it the case that in performing this basic speech act they were also doing something else, such as advising, or warning, or beseeching, or commanding, in virtue of some convention that is non-linguistic in nature? The question arises as a result of the observation, not uncommon in the course of studying the *Gītā*, that quite often the supposed answer to a query appears to have no apparent logical connection with the question that was being asked.* It is, as though, the sage went off on a different tangent from the one he was supposed to take, had he attended carefully to the precise nature of the query.

To the extent that the response can be clearly specified as a performative utterance it raises doubts about whether it is subject to truth or falsity.[2] If, however, the response is taken as a straightforward *statement* rather than a 'performative utterance' (in the original sense in which J.L. Austin used the phrase), then the question arises whether what has been stated is true or false. Evidently, by saying what the sage says he/she takes himself/herself to be stating something that is true. In that case, there must be assumed to be a method for ascertaining the truth or falsity of the statements. Before, however, inquiring into that method, it becomes imperative to analyse, clarify and elucidate what exactly it is that was being stated. The difficulty, which is a profound difficulty for a serious philosophic reader, is that, although words are being used to make an utterance, it is extremely difficult to decipher precisely what it is that has been said (in the sense of a *proposition* that has been asserted) intelligibly enough to allow one to proceed in the further enquiry. One cannot, in philosophic matters, take a sage's *saying* what he does to be true just because it is the *sage* who says it any more than one can take a statement in the Bible to be true on the sole grounds that it is the Bible that says it.

Very few, if any, of the philosophically significant utterances that one finds in the *Gītā* can be taken literally. They were never *meant* to be taken literally. The sages were extremely clever in that respect. They camouflaged the intentional content of their utterances very well, indeed. Sometimes too well, for their own good or, for that matter, for the good of anyone else. As a consequence, they have a positively obscure and opaque character. But this, I believe, was done quite intentionally. And I think they *knew* what they were doing and *why* they were doing it. Bertrand Russell's observation about the two distinguishable impulses in the history of philosophical thought is well known to those acquainted with his impressive little book on *Mysticism and Logic*. He calls them

*See, for example the question in the *Bhagvadgītā*, chap. ii, 54 and the response in chap. 11, 55-63.

the 'mystical impulse' and the 'logical' one. I think it is true that the reasons or the grounds for the sages' deliberate expression of what they had in mind, in an obscure and not easily decipherable or comprehensible form, was 'an expression of, if anything, the most extreme kind of 'logical impulse'. It was, indeed, 'a revolutionary attempt to encourage one to *think for oneself*; to challenge authority',[3] to discover the philosophical content of what they uttered by making a serious effort at philosophical thinking oneself rather than taking anyone's word for granted. Their rationale was that, unless one succeeded in understanding what it was that they were 'saying' (and they did not wish to make it easy), it was impossible to bring about the rational conviction that was the necessary condition, though not the sufficient one, for the possibility of its being *appropriated* in one's conduct. Wisdom was not a matter of learning and repeating what one is told by someone else, nor did it consist in following in detail any sort of injunctions laid down in the so-called 'holy books'. It consisted, for them, in conducting oneself in light of one's truly understanding one's own nature as well as the nature of everything that is the case in the world that one is faced with, and in grasping the nature of the interrelation between oneself and the rest of the universe.

But I am getting too far ahead. Let me address myself to one particular passage in the *Gītā* which seems to me to be centrally related to the general question that I had referred to earlier, namely, 'How should one live?' The passage occurs in the *Bhagvadgītā* chap. iv. 18. It is a well-known *śloka*, and there are numerous ways it has been rendered. I shall not concern myself with evaluating the accuracy and inaccuracy of one or another translation. The significant aspect of this passage is that the sage speaks of a person, namely, *buddhimān* (a person of wisdom, although this routine translation does not quite capture the full connotation of the Sanskrit term, there is no better alternative) as one who is not merely *capable* of conducting but *does* conduct himself in such a way that he is able to see (i.e. discern) action, (*karma*) in inaction (*akarma*) and inaction in action, or *akarma* in *karma*.

Now, of course, if one ponders about this statement seriously—and it is indeed a *statement*, for it makes a certain *assertion*—it creates a kind of mental cramp. This results from the paradoxical nature of the way in which it is expressed. A term 'action' and its opposite 'inaction' are being claimed to be interchangeable, and the *fact* that they *are* interchangeable and the *conditions* of this interchangeability are clearly discernible to one who is *buddhimān*, i.e. one who is exercising his *buddhi* (normally translated as 'intellect'). The cramp is the result of being unable to figure out, for oneself, what those conditions could be. It is like a riddle, but a fascinating one, especially for a philosopher. He finds himself in a labyrinth, and the only way to find a way out is to use a good deal of patience, thought and intelligence, and not run about every which way to find an escape. He can't do with an escape; what he needs is a solution, so that the labyrinth will no longer be a place of dread. Fortunately, and by calculated design, the sages have left several clues to finding one's way out. These clues are scattered throughout the *Gītā*. The difficulty is in deciding between the relevant and the irrelevant ones. The sages were infernally secretive individuals.

Now the term 'action' is used both as *karma* and *dharma* in a variety of senses in the *Gītā*. And it will lead nowhere but to a dead-end, if we concern ourselves with those senses that are connected with the notion of *vidhi* (i.e. a command, or precept or injunction) as one finds, for instance, in the *Pūrva Mimāṁsā* treatise. That sense of 'action' is concerned with the performance of ritualistic activities with a view to gaining a desired end for the sake of some benefit that is supposed to result from their performance. Such activities or 'actions', though their origin and justification may be of historical, sociological or anthropological interest, are entirely useless and irrelevant to the philosophical concept of action as related to the notion of *buddhi* in the passage under consideration. This philosophical notion needs to be understood without reference to any sort of ritual or custom or history.

The *Gītā* warns us rightly that the notions of 'action' and 'inaction' are so difficult to grasp that even intelligent people are confused about them (chap. iv. 16). The *Gītā* adds that there is not only *karma* and *akarma* but also *vikarma* or wrong action (chap. iv. 17). The introduction of the notion of *vikarma* is, I fear, made to lead one in the direction of a false clue, for an understanding of the notion of action (*karma*) logically implies an understanding of the nature of that to which the concept of action is *not* applicable.

That includes both inaction as well as wrong action. But what exactly counts as an action? Now in the *Gītā* a necessary relation is clearly suggested between the function of *buddhi* or intellect and the performance of what counts as an *action*. This being the case, the question arises as to what the exact function of the intellect is? And I would here suggest that it is *in principle* impossible (i.e. logically impossible) for the intellect (of a person) to be active on its *own* and in no way to be influenced by factors that impede its exercising its function, and yet make a false judgement. In other words, it is the very nature of the *buddhi* or intellect to understand things truly as they are without any distortion.

It has been rightly observed by Stuart Hampshire that action is attributable to a human being only as long as and throughout the period that he is conscious.

> It is a necessary truth—and one of the most important truisms about human beings—that if a man has been fully conscious for some time, there must be some verbs of action that truthfully summarise what he has been doing during that time. The verbs of action may represent him as doing something desultory, purposeless and inactive. The mode of performance may vary through many degrees: but if conscious, then necessarily performing, and if unconscious, necessarily not performing, in the sense that no action is attributable to an unconscious man as its agent. . . . A more decisive difference between consciousness and unconsciousness lies between the necessity of intended action in the one case and of a mere natural movement without intention in the other.[4]

I take Hampshire to be suggesting that non-intentional *action* is a logical impossibility. The sages of the *Gītā* do recognize this concept of action. When they speak of *naiṣkāmyakarma*, they do not, contrary to almost universally accepted opinion, mean 'desireless action'. For it is in principle impossible for behaviour to count as *action* unless the agent could answer the questions 'What were you doing?' and 'Why did you do it?' in terms of intention and desire, even if the answer to the second question were that one simply *wanted* to do it.

The sages of the *Gītā* assume that, in any instance of an action performed by a human being, it is always possible for the agent, if asked, to give an explanation of his behaviour by reference to those desires of which he is conscious. These desires, which are necessarily related to actions, are fundamentally emotive in character in the sense that they are *initiated* by various kinds of emotions generated through sense contacts with objects external to one's own body. Even in the absence of immediate direct sense contact, memories and associations connected with that contact are sufficient to give rise to the emotions originally generated through direct sense experience. Hence the suggestion that, since the actions are related to desires associated with emotions generated by sense experiences, some sort of a control of this process of sense contacts was a necessary condition of avoiding being affected by the emotions and desires that follow from them. This is perfectly reasonable. But there is the further suggestion, which is highly significant, that merely *avoidance* of the contact of senses with their objects is not enough. The individual must also be aware as to *why* this contact is to be avoided. The desire to avoid those emotions and desires that arise as a consequence of sense contacts is a second-order desire, distinct from first-order desires. Unless the *second-order* desire can be brought about, the possibility of an action being connected with such a desire (namely, the one modified by an understanding of the reasons for avoiding the first order desire) will have to be ruled out. It should be of interest to note that the importance which the *Gītā* sages placed upon the notion of 'second-order desire' (i.e. desire to have certain desires) for ethical reflection and practical consciousness has only recently been recognized in philosophical literature.[5] This indicates, on any account, an extraordinary philosophical insight on the part of those ancient sages who were engaged in philosophical thinking on this matter 1500 or 2000 years ago.

The *Gītā* sages suggested that the desire to avoid certain desires must be informed by a clear perception and recognition of the nature of the desires that one seeks to avoid. The agent must also formulate a conscious justification for this avoidance as a result of an exercise of *buddhi* (or intellect) whose function is to perceive things exactly for what they are. It is also, they hold, the function of the *buddhi* to *evaluate* and *discriminate* between that which is merely pleasant and that which is good.[6] And it is only that desire (or those desires), which is connected with the active *buddhi* and is directed by the idea of the *good* rather than that of pleasure, that can give rise to action in the genuine sense of that term. Everything else falls into the category of 'inaction'. But, sadly enough, it is the category of 'inaction' that is ordinarily but mistakenly conceived to be the sphere of action by the unthinking multitude. For that is the 'action' that is guided by a desire connected with (the emotion of) pleasure and the avoidance of pain. From the point of view of one, who is solely governed in his actions by the desire for pleasure, the action of the individual informed by a discriminating *buddhi* that rejects such desires as appropriate for action would amount to an instance of *inaction*. To put in another way, what *in fact* amounts to *inaction* (*akarma*) would appear to a person with a non- (or mal-) functioning *buddhi* as an instance of *action* (*karma*); and what, in fact, amounts to *action* would appear to him as an instance of *inaction*. The sages of the *Gītā* point out that a truly intelligent individual whose *buddhi* or intellect is functioning properly would see that that which people uninformed by the *buddhi* consider to be inaction is genuinely an instance of action, and that which they *take* to be an action is genuinely an instance of inaction.

Now, perhaps, one begins to get a grasp of what the sage in the *Gītā* means and his reasons for saying 'one who sees action in inaction and inaction in action is wise among men' (chap. iv. 18).

NOTES

1. Bimal K. Matilal, 'Mysticism and Reality: Ineffability' in *Journal of Indian Philosophy*, vol. 3 September-December 1975, p. 246.
2. See G.J. Warnock in *Essays on J.L. Austin*, Oxford, 1973, pp. 69-90. I agree with Warnock who has convincingly argued that, despite some philosopher's attempt to undermine Austin's distinction between statements and performatives and Austin's own second thoughts about it, the original distinction that rests on the presence or absence of non-linguistic *conventions* in virtue of which certain utterances *count as* doing this or that does not break down on any ground.
3. J.H. Hattiangadi, 'Why is Indian Philosophy Mystical?' in *Journal of Indian Philosophy*, vol. 3. September-December 1975, p. 254.
4. See Stuart Hampshire, *Thought and Action*, London, Chatto and Windus, 1959, pp. 93-94.
5. See, for instance, H. Frankfurt, 'Freedom of the Will and the Concept of a Person', in *Journal of Philosophy*, 67, 1971; Amartya Sen, 'Choice, Order-

ings and Morality' in Stephen Koerner (ed.), *Practical Reason*, New Haven, Yale University Press, 1974; R.C. Jeffery, 'Preferences among Preferences' in *Journal of Philosophy*, 71, 1974; A.O. Hirschman, *Shifting Involvements* (chap. 4), Princeton, Princeton University Press, 1982. B. Williams, *Ethics and the Limits of Philosophy*, London, Fordham Press, 1985. Among the not so recent philosophers, I suspect that Spinoza had an inkling of the importance of the second-order desires for the concept of action.

6. See *Katha Upaniṣad* I.2.1 to I.2.4. These passages clearly point to a distinction made by the sages between the good (*śreya*) and the pleasant (*preya*), and they connect the notion of *buddhi* with the function of distinguishing between the two, and the *buddhimān* as one who prefers the good to the pleasant.

ARJUNA'S MORAL PREDICAMENT

M.M. AGRAWAL

THE appearance of moral dilemmas of grave human significance has been a perennial feature of the human situation. Anyone who is seriously interested in answering practical moral questions, especially in an older and pluralistic civilization such as ours, is bound to find himself, at least occasionally, in a situation where he seems morally obliged to do two different acts. But for some reason he cannot do both. It may sometimes be the case that doing one directly opposes the other, as, for example, inflicting capital punishment opposes giving a chance to the criminal to reform himself. At other times, it may be simply because it is physically impossible to realize both, as, for example, it is not possible to go and fight for one's country and at the same time stay back home to look after one's old and ailing mother. Naturally, then, in the philosophical history of ethics, there have always been debates on the nature of moral conflicts, even though the majority of the philosophers seem to have held the view that moral dilemmas are only apparent. Thus, Aristotle's famous doctrine of the unity of the virtues implies that there can be no conflict among the virtues.[1] In fact, in modern Western philosophy, both among the followers of Kant and the utilitarians, the dominant view has been to the effect that moral dilemmas are illusory. That is, they have believed that, in a given situation, morality cannot make two incompatible demands on the moral agent. In the case of Kant, since his fundamental moral principle is derived from human reason, the existence of moral dilemmas would amount to an internal incoherence within reason. For the utilitarians, who subsume all other moral principles under the principle of the greatest happiness of the greatest number, a moral dilemma is like a technical problem. It is only a question of working out accurately which of the horns of an apparent moral dilemma will actually produce the greatest happiness for the greatest number. But more recently several philosophers have challenged this belief.[2] The aim of this paper is not to defend or challenge the belief in question as such. It is to discuss a particular dilemma in the *Mahābhārata* and to assess if it has actually been resolved. We could then perhaps make some useful comments concerning moral dilemmas in general.

Before proceeding to our main task, however, some general observations will not be out of place. It is clear from the start that no one else can tell you, on grounds of principle, what you ought to do when in a dilemma. For whichever course of action one recommends, it will have to be backed by some moral theory or other. But, *ex hypothesi*, it is seen that there are compelling arguments for both horns of a dilemma. Indeed, one is confronted with a moral dilemma in the first place, partly because one is already operating within a framework of diverse moral viewpoints. That is why I said earlier that, in an older and pluralistic society which has inherited heterogeneous ethical cultures (i.e. belief systems relevant to moral decision making), one is likely to be more frequently placed in the situation of a moral dilemma.

How then does one proceed to resolve a moral dilemma? Does one simply toss a coin, or take a *decision*? Or is there a rational solution of the problem? It does seem that, if there is any hope of making a rationally satisfying choice, then there has to be a higher-order set of fundamental values, or principles embodying these values, by reference to which our diverse ethical viewpoints may be reconciled. Thus, in the final analysis, it may turn out that one of the obligations constituting the dilemma is not really a *moral* obligation; or, alternatively, that the other is at least seen to be a superior obligation. But this approach does not provide a solution for all the dilemma situations. For it always remains possible that the ultimate value or principle may be exemplified in both the obligatory acts constituting a dilemma. And, again, a more serious difficulty may arise, since the same independent and objective order of values may yield different moral theories, which, in turn, entail opposing obligations in the same situation. This may come about, since, as MacIntyre notes in what he calls the 'Sophoclean' view, 'there *is* an objective moral order, but our perceptions of it are such that we cannot bring rival moral truths into complete harmony with each other'.[3] The possibility, however, of moral conflict arising within *one* moral theory is no less remote. Although, as noted earlier, the dominant views in modern times preach some kind of monism, in which all apparent moral conflicts can in principle be resolved by reference to a single ultimate moral principle, other moral traditions, such as British intuitionism, have accepted the possibility of greater diversity. Richard Price denies that the ultimate single virtue 'consists in BENEVOLENCE' and claims six different virtues to be self-evidently ultimate.[4] In any case, throughout the history of mankind actual ethical conflicts have always stimulated fresh thinking on the questions of right and wrong, and have helped to advance human civilization. One such conflict, arising in the mind of Arjuna presenting a moral dilemma for him, is depicted in the *Mahābhārata* in the story of the battle of Kurukṣetra. Arjuna had come to the battlefield with every intention of fighting a deadly war in order to regain the kingdom from the Kauravas, the kingdom of which he was the rightful heir, and which the Kauravas in violence to *dharma* were, in fact, controlling and unwilling to part with. The principle of natural justice obliged Arjuna to regain the kingdom by force. This obligation was also endorsed by the assured expectations of the ruled to have a just state under the rule of the rightful ruler. When, however, the stage is set for a battle, Arjuna, facing the warriors whom he is supposed to destroy, is suddenly struck by a crippling emotion of grief at the thought of having to kill the opponents before him. A moral conflict is set in his mind, and he begins to doubt the very validity of the whole enterprise. Should he or should he not fight the war is the question haunting his mind. He finally succumbs to his doubts and submits to Kṛṣṇa, his philosopher and guide, that he cannot and ought not to fight as he thinks it better to surrender his rights rather than kill his kinsmen opposing him. Arjuna's loyalty to the cause of justice and the happiness of his immediate family comes in direct conflict with his goodwill towards his kinsmen in general and other traditional virtues such as loyalty to one's tribe as a whole, respect for elders and gurus (who were among the opponents), and so on. Let us then look at the shift in Arjuna's thinking in some detail.

Arjuna's scepticism is a typical example of how moral conflict arises in times of crisis when in our ordinary intuitive moral thinking we rely on utilitarian principles. But intuition is unable to resolve the conflict. We have to undertake a critical utilitarian assessment of the situation. But can impartial critical utilitarian considerations resolve the dilemma?

Arjuna has obviously arrived at the battlefield with every intention of fighting after having duly considered the situation in consultation with others concerned. His reasons for fighting are connected with a moral theory which gets its meaning from the notion of an ideal society (*rāmrājya*) in which the principle of justice must be upheld at all costs. Arjuna has characterized the opponents as unjust and as criminal.[5] He sees that they are filled with greed, and have geared themselves to this horrible war for the sake of their personal gratification.[6] Thus, Arjuna is in no doubt about the unworthiness of the Kauravas' ambitions and the legitimacy of his own right to kill them. Yet a doubt has crept into his mind. Is it really worth it? Standing on the battle field face to face with his opponents it has suddenly dawned upon him (though he must have already known it) that the battle involves killing his own kinsmen, his affectionate friends, his respected elders, and revered gurus. His initial response is highly emotional: 'I do not wish to kill them, even for the gain of the kingdom of all the three worlds.'[7] But later he reasons from the point of view of self-interest. He says that he does not envisage any personal happiness at regaining the kingdom when all his near and dear ones have been killed. One cannot enjoy any gain at such a cost. 'Having slayed my own kinsmen and so on, what shall I do with the kingdom and the pleasures of life?'[8] But there is much more to Arjuna's reasoning. There now follows a whole lot of solid *moral* reasons for the shift in his attitude. These reasons seem to be connected with a different moral theory from the one suggested in favour of his earlier decision to fight. It is a theory which gets its meaning and purpose from a social context which was very real in Arjuna's cultural milieu. The traditional obligations which he now invokes are embedded in a way of life in which the loyalty to one's clan, the happiness of one's kinsmen and friends, and respect for one's elders and gurus seems to be considered the most important. Thus, notwithstanding the legitimacy of his right to kill the Kauravas, Arjuna argues on moral grounds that a family fight, since it leads to disastrous consequences for the whole clan, must be avoided. The battle is definitely going to destroy the clan, and such a battle is evidently evil. And the killing of friends and elders is clearly sinful. Moreover, Arjuna who, unlike the Kauravas, sees the bizarre future consequences of the war has a further reason for avoiding the fight. He makes the point that, while the Kauravas have a limited vision of the war and ignore the horrors to come, 'we who understand the evils of such a war must try to avoid it'.[9] Arjuna then goes on in some detail to trace the sequence of the consequences of the war in question as follows.[10]

In the death of the elders and the gurus of the clan the structure of authority in the clan is destroyed. Then there follows the decline of moral order in the clan. From this decline comes the corruption of the women of the family. This, in turn, leads to racial/caste intermixture and impurity in the whole clan, which leads them all to hell. And, further, since they are no longer offering *piṇda* to the deceased ancestors, they also suffer a fall in their spiritual status and perhaps remain in limbo. And, further, the numerous evils generated by racial/caste impurity lead to the destruction of the established caste morality as well as clan morality, that is, of the moral order in society as a whole. The decline of moral order in society brings ruin and unhappiness to all, sending all of them finally to hell.

From the above account we can see now, while Arjuna's dilemma is partly based upon a conflict of sentiments and partly of prudence, it is primarily a *moral* dilemma. Arjuna makes it clear that, among other things, the consequences of the war will be to produce the greatest unhappiness for the greatest number concerned. He is then alluding to the well-known utilitarian standard of morality expressed in our times by Bentham as 'the greatest good of the greatest number'. But the considerations leading to the original determination of his will to fight seem to be invoking another, perhaps a Kantian type of standard of doing one's duty for the sake of duty, while what is one's duty is not determined in the first place by utility but by existing moral *practices* within a society. So Arjuna is appealing to a plurality of moral standards. And some of his remarks seems to imply that in his society each clan and caste had its own set of moral duties, presumably derived from the same moral standard and harmonized in some kind of moral 'whole'. And yet there obviously exists a dynamic tension between them. In Arjuna's view, the breakdown of moral authority in one clan can seriously disrupt the balance between sectional moralities and cause a chaos in the society as a whole. For all these undesirable consequences Arjuna considers himself personally accountable, and, therefore, takes a moral stand. Finally, it is to be noted that the total picture of the calamities due to the war drawn by Arjuna does involve not only the present and the future generations but also the deceased ancestors. His then is a thoroughly utilitarian argument demanding the sacrifice of his personal gains for the sake of the happiness of all.

Normally, one would expect that a rationally acceptable moral code would not include incompatible duties, and consequently would not generate moral dilemmas. Arjuna's conflict, as we have seen, is not only a conflict of sentiments but also a conflict of moral standards. There are, it seems, as a matter of fact, a plurality of moral values and standards; and, life being what it is, they sometimes command conflicting actions. Moreover, as Lemmon puts it: 'there are generally different ways in which it can come to be true that we ought to do something or not to do something'.[11] He explains that a conflict may arise due to the fact that what a person ought to do may be based on his status or position by reference to his previous commitments, or on certain moral principles. And these can conflict. Something like this also seems to be true in the case of Arjuna's conflict. As a Kṣatriya prince, he ought to fight to regain the kingdom of which he is the rightful heir. On the other hand, the utilitarian principle of 'the greatest good of the greatest number' recommends to him not to fight. Thus, the manifest diversity of human values inevitably leads to a moral conflict. It is, however, often suggested that it is possible to connect the conflicting values to some one supreme value, as, for example, what the utilitarians attempt. Or, alternatively, it is argued that within the broad division between moral and non-moral values the specifically moral values have priority over other values, and the spectrum of moral values merges into a single supreme moral value. However, it is not at all easy to prove any of these positions supporting moral monism. For one thing, it is not always possible to draw a sharp line between moral and non-moral values. For instance, is the loyalty expected of one due to the fact that one belongs to a certain religious community a moral obligation or not? I am sure that different philosophers will answer differently. Next, some of the obligations do not seem to be derived from any higher value at all. For example, some find it intuitively certain that they have certain duties towards their parents simply because of the fact of their unique relationship. These duties are not derived from any higher moral value. But they are self-evidently moral duties, and in certain situations they may clash with other equally moral duties which are required to be performed.

KṚṢṆA'S RESPONSE

Keeping the above-mentioned complexity of moral obligation in mind, let us see how Kṛṣṇa attempts to resolve the dilemma in question. His initial response in order to satisfy Arjuna on all the three counts, namely, emotional, prudential, and ethical, appears to provide an odd mixture of moral and non-moral reasons. But, as his discourse develops, its moral character begins to dominate. Converting a mere family fight (in Arjuna's conception) into a *dharmayuddha*, Kṛṣṇa considers Arjuna's conflict basically as a moral dilemma.

On the emotional front, Kṛṣṇa admonishes Arjuna for his weakness of the will. He characterizes Arjuna's state of mind as of *moha*, i.e. sentimental attachment. Such a state of mind deprives one of heavenly happiness and bestows notoriety upon one.[12] Kṛṣṇa condemns Arjuna for harbouring unmanly emotion which blinds one to one's own interests, weakens one for action, and blurs one's discriminative abilities making him like a dead man. Kṛṣṇa spends a long time preaching that it is irrational to lament for the death of the body. The message is brought home finally by invoking the esoteric doctrines of the immortality of the soul and rebirth. The essential being of a person, the soul, is declared indestructible. After each death it is reborn. It casts away bodies like a man who discards old clothes and gets new ones.[13] It is unworthy to feel attachment for the body, when the soul that 'wears' it is everlasting. A wise man does not identify himself with his body.

Next, Kṛṣṇa argues that to allow oneself to be swayed by the emotion of grief and feel crippled by *moha* is clearly imprudent, for the inaction it recommends will bring one countless personal losses.[14] He tells Arjuna that if he does not fight

(*a*) People will call him a coward and he will lose honour and respect in the eyes of others;
(*b*) By failing to do what he is capable of as a warrior he will be losing the pleasures of life now and also the heavenly abode of the afterlife;
(*c*) On the other hand, if he is killed in this war, he will definitely go to heaven, and, if he wins, he will inherit the earth.

Having pointed out all these rewards for fighting, Kṛṣṇa now quietly shifts his reasoning to the spiritual plane. He observes that the wise man remains calm through the drama of pleasures and pains. He does not lament a personal loss, nor rejoice in the gains; for both of these are irrelevant to the blissful being of the eternal self.

In his specifically moral reasoning Kṛṣṇa, declares the war to be a *dharmayuddha*, i.e. a righteous or just war. While Arjuna, though in doubt about the injustice done to him, had come to fight with the motive of personal gain of the kingdom, Kṛṣṇa makes it clear that for a man in his position it was a moral obligation to fight.[15] Such a war, far from being a sin, is the gateway to heaven. Rather, not fighting, i.e. not fulfilling his obligation, will involve him in sin and responsibility for all its terrible consequence.[16] Moreover, there is nothing distinctively moral in acting with the motive of personal gain. Since one has right only to action and not to its 'fruits', one ought to act in non-attachment to the consequences of one's actions.[17]

Thus, the overall character of Kṛṣṇa's argument is clearly ethical. Its force is to the effect that a righteous war must be fought independently of considerations of personal gain or loss. This war is righteous, since it aims at justice which is the very foundation of human existence. Arjuna in his status as a warrior-prince has a moral duty to fight such a war. In this he must ignore the demands of his attachments. And, even though, as a matter of fact, fighting this war will bring him personal gain, he must not fight *for the sake of* these gains. To maintain its distinctively moral worth, Arjuna must fight with the motive of duty alone. This he can ensure, only if he has risen from the state of *moha* to the state of non-attachment. Thus, the utilitarian reasons of Arjuna for not fighting have been interrogated by a sort of Kantian ethics of duty.

REVIEW OF THE NATURE OF ARJUNA'S CONFLICT

If, in a given situation, two different sets of reasons, both prima facie equally good, dictate two different obligations, and it is not possible to enact both, nor to eliminate one by reference to a higher-order principle, and yet in actual life one has to choose one, then it is clear that one has to suppress one's propensity to realize one in favour of the other quite arbitrarily. And, for this reason, one is likely to feel remorse. In such cases, as Williams rightly suggests, moral conflicts are like conflicts of desire.[18] And, further, he says, just as suppressing one desire in favour of the other one does of the former, by ignoring one moral obligation for the sake of fulfilling the other one has not really resolved the conflict. One has simply gone ahead despite the conflict. Thus, unlike conflicts of belief, in moral conflicts a moral 'reminder' remains uneliminable and is shown by the fact that one feels remorse for not being able to carry out the ignored 'ought'. Now, Arjuna's conflict turns out to illustrate this point clearly. For, as Kṛṣṇa suspects, Arjuna's primary motive in contemplating surrender is to give vent to his sentiments, and the cause of this lies in his attachments. True, Arjuna gives solid moral reasons in support of his revised attitude. But then, earlier, he had equally good reasons for contemplating killing the very same people whom he now thinks he cannot and should not kill. In adopting this new attitude, he has simply suppressed his earlier decision. But, as we have said, abandoning one horn of the dilemma in favour of the other does not dissolve the conflict. What, one might ask, *justifies* Arjuna's shift in his attitude? For simply stating a new set of reasons implying a contrary obligation does not show that his earlier reasons were morally inferior. And Arjuna has done nothing to prove that they are. He has simply given new reasons to support his revised attitude. Indeed, his new attitude is dictated by his sentiments and attachments. And the fact that he adduces new reasons to justify his new attitude towards the war is secondary, and is itself determined by his sentiments. His reasons may be good reasons, but the ground for drawing upon a new set of reasons instead of sticking to the earlier ones is itself a-rational; it is rooted in his affections and fears. That is, his moral dilemma springs not simply from a conflict between two different sets of reasons, both valid in the situation, but also from an inheritance of conflicting values and their accompanying sentiments in his psyche.

In general, our sentiments and fears cannot be divorced from what we value and the reasons we, in fact, give to support our practical decisions. A dilemma situation is only a special case of a situation in which one has to decide between different alternatives. For the same situation could, in principle, depending upon our sentiments, desires and dispositions, elicit different interpretations and consequently set in motion different chains of reasons yielding different 'oughts'. And if the conflicting 'oughts' cannot be brought under one overriding principle, then we have a moral dilemma. So, given that there is no one absolute, objective and integrated set of ultimate moral principles, reason alone cannot resolve a moral dilemma. In the case of a complex moral conflict as deep as that of Arjuna's, in which a whole way of life is challenged, the way out is not simply to abandon one 'ought' and opt for the other on the strength of one's present intuitive appreciation of the depth of the reasons supporting them. For, as we have seen, the strength of one's present conviction alone does not prove that the earlier conviction was morally inferior. Rather, an arbitrary choice will be considered degenerate in a way in which his present state is not, since, although conflicting, it is at least rooted in his own experience of life, and, therefore, expresses his real choices. For an authentic resolution of the conflict, it is necessary that one does not simply ignore one part of the conflict, but that it be purged out of one's psyche from its very roots. And, further, the alternative which is expelled is actually apprehended as morally inferior or in some sense illusory. And, again, if the choice has been made by reference to a new discovery of an ultimate principle, then the discovery must be of the nature of a radical conversion, a total transformation of one's outlook on life. And the new outlook must be self-evidently morally superior.

THE TRUE RESOLUTION OF ARJUNA'S CONFLICT

What is most interesting and important in Kṛṣṇa's approach to the resolution of the conflict is precisely this: that finally Kṛṣṇa is able to affect the relevant kind of radical conversion or enlightenment. From what we have said so far it is clear that Kṛṣṇa's response to Arjuna on the three counts, namely, emotional, prudential, and ethical, has more or less had the effect of simply underlining, in a more articulate way, Arjuna's earlier judgements and attitudes. By providing Arjuna with good reasons for sticking to his earlier decision, Kṛṣṇa has not really resolved his dilemma. His task is still incomplete. For, although he has correctly identified the cause of Arjuna's dejection and the motive behind the shift in his attitude, he has not shown that Arjuna's new stand is morally unjustified.

Kṛṣṇa now realizes that to get Arjuna out of the dilemma he has to make him look at the situation in a completely new way. Both Arjuna's judgements, the earlier and the revised, regarding the desirability of the battle are made within a frame of reference which reflects an incomplete picture of reality. The picture is not radically incoherent, rather it contains blemishes that are corrigible. Arjuna's conflicting interpretation of the situation shows his ignorance of the underlying reality which supports it. Kṛṣṇa seems to believe that, if only Arjuna could see the imminent battle in the context of the whole of cosmic reality, he would emerge from his confused state of mind and take the right decision. For this reason, Kṛṣṇa enlarges the scope of his discourse to cover the area of transcendental knowledge. Kṛṣṇa explains the underlying unity of cosmic reality, including the nature of such things as the self, death and the creation of cosmic beings, matter and mind, action and predestination, etc. The casuistic resources of Kṛṣṇa's discourse tends to correct Arjuna's ontological worldview. But, while the discourse may have altered many of Arjuna's beliefs about the situation he was in, it was not sufficient to change his sentiments and fears which, we have seen, were the basic determinants of the shift in his reasoning. No doubt beliefs do limit the range of one's desires, and make one consider some fears as baseless and some sentiments as unnecessary. But beliefs by themselves cannot eliminate these, and transform one's total sense of values. In order to affect that transformation, one needs the impact of first-hand experience and knowledge of the highest kind. Thus, in the present case, the relevant experience cannot be of any ordinary kind, but somewhat different, although nevertheless within the empirical framework of mundane life; for the conflicting axiological frame of reference of Arjuna's dilemma is already a residue of the richness and the variety of his experience of life. It is because Arjuna is an 'insider' *vis-à-vis* this frame of thought that he is a victim of the dilemma in the first place. For him to be able to perceive his situation as a whole he has to step outside the present experiential framework. And this is precisely what is made available to Arjuna in a vision of cosmic reality. In this Arjuna perceives the entire process of cosmic creation and destruction. He sees how individual souls are involved in the order of nature and what it would mean to attain spiritual freedom. He sees the true nature of thought, action, emotion, etc. Seeing all this, his attachment to mortal existence is destroyed, and the sentiments and fears consequent upon his attachment disappear. He is free from *moha*, and relinquishing all thoughts of personal gain he is now in a position to act from the motive of duty alone.

How exactly the perception of the 'whole', the vision affects this transformation in Arjuna is not easy to understand. There is obviously no strictly logical step from what one experiences to what one values and desires. Nevertheless, it is not impossible to guess what may have happened. Since the vision is a totally new experience, it must produce structural changes in the subject's psyche, resulting in a significantly new orientation of the mind. So, realizing not only intellectually but deeply, existentially, that the inner self is immortal, Arjuna now feels no grief at the thought of the death of his affectionate and respected ones. Similarly, seeing that the war is inevitable and that he is only instrumental to it, Arjuna no longer fears killing his elders. And, realizing that in acting without the motive of personal gain one stands outside the order of causes and effects, he no longer fears that he will be infected by sin in killing the elders, etc. The result of this new orientation of mind is that certain considerations drop out as *irrelevant* in determining how to act. Thus, for example, the fact that Arjuna's dear ones will die in the war becomes irrelevant to the question of fighting a righteous war. Similarly, in the light of the revelation of the true nature of the self and its implication in the order of causes, the fact that the immediate consequences of the war will be hellish appears insignificant. And, further, Arjuna's earlier emotions and the reasons they suggested are rendered irrelevant.

It is, therefore, not unreasonable to assume that, from the vantage point of truth, the enlightened man's mind will embrace only *one* set of values, and that that one set of values must be internally coherent, and must somehow reflect the true and eternal order in nature. Since it is impossible for the natural intelligence of man to believe that reality is internally incoherent, it is impossible for reason to accept that the same reality, when lived and directly experienced, will imprint upon the enlightened mind a set of con flicting values and sentiments.

The principle that the perception of truth alone is sufficient to bring about a total transformation of the human psyche has been upheld in all the major branches of Indian spiritual philosophy. Furthermore, the enlightened being is characterized as a 'free' being. In the state of spiritual freedom, the mind of the individual is identical with the mind of God, or, what amounts to the same thing, the individual merges into the Divine; and, therefore, in his actions, he is no longer guided by the limitations of his individual ego. It is, therefore, not difficult to see that an enlightened man must be free from all conflicts of beliefs as well as of emotions, and would naturally will *one* thing. Then there would be no room for a moral dilemma. Further, it is needless to defend the moral superiority of the decisions taken in the state of spiritual freedom. On the attainment of enlightenment, involving total understanding of human existence, man has reached the culmination of his spiritual evolution. When a man acts from the standpoint of truth, how could his action not be morally supreme?

We are now in a position to make the following comment on Kṛṣṇa's ethical standpoint. He does vindicate an ethical monism, but a qualified one. It is suggested that, so long as our knowledge is limited to the empirical world, we are not in a position to grasp the ultimate ethical significance of a given situation and the choices we make in it. From our limited point of view, neither intuition nor reason nor the principle of utility can ensure that no genuine moral dilemmas will arise. But when our knowledge is extended to the eternal order of causes, and one understands the fundamental structures of human existence, then, from that vision of truth, one is in no doubt as to which action is morally supreme. The understanding works on our reason through the resolution of conflicts in our emotions. Virtue is necessary to moral choice, and enlightenment is necessary for virtue.

NOTES

1. See Aristotle, *The Nicomachean Ethics*, tr. W.D. Ross, Oxford, Oxford University Press, 1980.
2. See, for example, A. MacIntyre, *After Virtue: A Study in Moral Theory*, Notre Dame, University of Notre Dame Press, 1981.
3. *Ibid.*, p. 134.
4. Richard Price 'A Review of the Principal Questions in Morals' in *British Moralists*, ed., D.D. Raphael, vol. 2 Oxford, Oxford University Press, 1969, p. 176.
5. *The Gīta*, chap. 1, verse 36. (In all subsequent references to the *Gīta* only chapter and verse numbers are given.
6. 1.38.
7. 1.35.
8. 1.32.
9. 1.38-39.
10. 1.40-44.
11. E.J. Lemmon, 'Moral Dilemmas' in *Moral Dilemmas*, ed. Christopher W. Gowans, New York, Oxford University Press, 1987, p. 105.
12. 2.2.
13. 2.22.
14. 2.33-37.
15. 2.31.
16. 2.33.
17. 2.47.
18. Bernard, Williams, 'Ethical Consistency', in *Moral Dilemmas*, ed. Christopher W. Gowans, New York ,Oxford University Press, 1987.

ARJUNAVIṢĀDAYOGA

E. R. SREEKRISHNA SARMA

A pathetic and pessimistic scene is described towards the end of the great epic, the seventy-eighth chapter of the Āśvamedhika-parvan in the *Mahābhārata.* It is well known, as the great poet Ānandavardhana points out in his *Dhvanyāloka* (Kākā 5), that the great war disillusioned both the parties that fought it, everybody finding himself or herself plunged into utter confusion and despair. *Mahāmuninā vairāgyajananatātparyam prādhānyena svaprabandhasya darṣayatā mokṣalakṣaṇah puruṣārthaḥ santo rasas ca mukhyatayā vivaksāvisayatvena sucitaḥ.* All were sorrowful, the victors as well as the vanquished. Perhaps the victors were more sorrowful since they had to continue living in this world. As Duryodhana said at the time of his death, abondoning their intentions they have to live in sorrow '*Yuyamvihatasamkalpāḥ śocanto vartayisyatha*' (Śalyaparvan, 60, 50). Dhṛtarāṣṭra, the king and the head of the Kauravas, was in deep sorrow because of the loss of his sons and dear ones. Yudhiṣṭhira, the eldest of the Pāṇḍavas, was in utter confusion. He did not know what to do next. Seeing him in that pessimistic mood his brothers sat around him, and even Dhṛtarāṣṭra came to console him. Taking a hint from Kṛṣṇa, Vyāsa suggested he should perform the sacrifice of Aśvamedha to wash away the great sin of causing the destruction of so many lives. The sage also suggested to him to send Arjuna along to protect the sacrificial horse. Yudhiṣṭhira agreed to the suggestions, and decided to perform the Aśvamedha sacrifice. Vyāsa also told him not to worry about the great expenditure; no new tax would be levied from the subjects. A lot of wealth had been accumulated by Marutta in the Himalayas. Marutta was a king born in the line of Ikṣvāku who performed one hundred Aśvamedha sacrifices, and prepared Kuṇḍas and vessels with gold with the grace of Parameśvara whom he propitiated with his penance. This wealth could be used by Yudhiṣṭhira now. It was expected that normally there would be no serious resistance from the kings. Yet, the relatives of those who were killed in the battle bore a grudge against the Pāṇḍavas, and they put up stiff resistance to Arjuna by fighting. Of course, Arjuna could subdue the kings who resisted him, and he proceeded victoriously from country to country. In the course of time, he reached the Saindhava kingdom which was formerly ruled by Jayadratha and now by his son Suratha.

Jayadratha was the son-in-law of Dhṛtarāṣṭra. He fought for the Kauravas in the war, and played a vital role in killing Abhimanyu, the heroic son of Arjuna. Arjuna at that time made a pledge to slay Jayadratha the next day before sunset. The Kaurava fighters put up a stiff resistance, but Arjuna could redeem his pledge with the help of a trick played by Kṛṣṇa. When the sun was about to set on that day, the Kauravas were in high spirits. Jayadratha was looking at the setting sun, while Kṛṣṇa suddenly asked Arjuna to slay him on the spot. But slaying Jayadratha was not an easy task. His head should not fall on the ground, for if this happened, the head of the killer would burst into a hundred pieces. This was because of a curse pronounced by Vṛddhakṣatra, the father of Jayadratha. Vṛddhakṣatra had no issue for a long time. He propitiated Śiva and obtained his favour. When Jayadratha was born there was a concealed voice (*aśarīrī*) that the boy would grow into a brave fighter, but would be slain by a renowned enemy in battle. Vṛddhakṣatra was perturbed by the voice. He immediately pronounced the curse that whoever in the battle causes Jayadratha's head to fall on the ground would immediately die, his head bursting into a hundred pieces. Kṛṣṇa knew this secret, and advised Arjuna to make the head fall on the lap of Vṛddhakṣatra who was doing penance nearby in the Himalayas. Arjuna's skill in archery could accomplish this rare feat. With his arrow he not only cut the head of Jayadratha but his successive arrows made the head fall on the lap of Vṛddhakṣatra who was in deep meditation and did not notice it. When he came out of his meditation and stood up, the head rolled down to the ground. He could see the head of his son with two brightly shining earrings for a moment, and immediately his head burst into a hundred pieces. This is how Vṛddhakṣatra became the victim of his own terrible curse.

The warriors in the Sindhu country put up a tough fight to Arjuna, although he was able finally to subdue them. After that Arjuna was resting on his laurels. He then noticed a woman carrying an infant child coming towards him. A close look revealed her to be Duḥśalā, the only daughter of Dhṛtarāṣṭra and Gāndhārī and the only sister of the warriors of the Kaurava race. Duḥśalā was born to Gāndhārī as the hundred and first child. Seeing his sister coming in a desperate mood the weapons fell down from Arjuna's hand. He stood up and asked her with love and humility what she wanted. She told him that after Jayadratha, her husband, was killed in the war, his son Suratha became the king of the Sindhus. Hearing the news that Arjuna, his father's killer, was coming to the country as the protector of the Aśvamedha-horse, Suratha was terribly frightened and died instantaneously out of fear. The child in her arms was Suratha's. She wanted to beg for the protection of this child. This was why she had come.

Now Arjuna began to remember the past. Who was Duḥśalā? Gāndhārī desired to have a hundred valiant sons who would win over their enemies and rule over the kingdom. Vyāsa told her that she would have them. Later Gāndhārī thought that she would have a daughter to be the sister of her sons. She became pregnant and love the foetus for two years. Meanwhile she came to know that Kuntī, the wife of Pāṇḍu, had given birth to a bright male child. The news made Gāndhārī envious and impatient. She also was tired of bearing the child for such a long time. Her impatience disturbed her womb and a huge lump of flesh came out. She became worried and wanted to throw it away. Just then Vyāsa came there and told her that his words would be fulfilled. She would get a hundred valiant sons. He advised her to wash the lump of flesh with cold water. When washed it split into a hundred pieces. Vyāsa asked her to prepare a hundred pots filled with ghee and put each piece in a pot. After filling a hundred pots in this way, there was one piece remaining. From the pots came out babies one by one beginning with Duryodhana. The last piece came out as a female child which was named

Duḥśalā. She was married to Jayadratha, the king of the Sindhus. When Abhimanyu entered the lotus formation (*padmavyūha*) arranged by Droṇa, Jayadratha encountered the Pāṇḍavas, keeping all the veterans at bay, thus making way for the great fighters to kill Abhimanyu. This was the cause of the enmity between Arjuna and Jayadratha. Of course, Arjuna had revenge for the crime by slaying Jayadratha the next day.

Duḥśalā also implored Arjuna to protect his sister's child as he would do in the case of Abhimanyu's new-born child. Abhimanyu's child Pārīkṣit was protected by Kṛṣṇa when the Brahmāstra of Aśvatthāmā entered the womb of Uttarā to destroy the foetus.

Let us for a moment imagine the mental state of Arjuna at that time. Any human being meeting a young woman such a stale, would be embarrassed and distressed. And this was his own sister and he was himself the cause of her misery. The situation was unbearable. His thoughts must have gone like this. We, the Pāṇḍavas, have reached an enviable position in this world by eliminating all the enemies and securing a vast kingdom. But the result of our heroic deeds is that the only sister of the one hundred and five Kaurava brothers has been reduced to the condition of a beggar with her grandson in her arms. She is the only daughter of our uncle Dhṛtarāṣṭra who looked after us when we grew up, our father having passed away quite a few years earlier. Our uncle was loving and kind towards us, though he had one weak point in that he was very fond of his sons and could never prevent them from doing wrong. Was he to blame? As for our aunt Gāndhārī, the mother of Duḥśalā, she was innocent of that weakness. Suppose, even one among the hundred brothers who lost their lives due to their greed for riches and glories were to be alive today, would he be able the bear this pathetic sight? Even if we lay all the riches and glories we have earned at her feet, would it compensate for the sins we have committed? It is true that some of her brothers did the shameful act of dragging her brothers' wife Pāñcālī to an open assembly and insulted her modesty by their shameful conduct. But all her husbands, we five were present and witnessed it, and we could have prevented it had we the resolution. But, in the case of this pitiable woman, there is none to save her. Should I not feel the same sense of shame and insult to *dharma* now, as ought to have been felt by Duryodhana and his associates on that occasion? This woman's husband, of course, played a vital role in killing my heroic son Abhimanyu, and I have, indeed, retaliated by killing him before the sun set next day. Then, who would do the heinous crime of killing his son? But this is what has happened, even though I had no wish for it. The mother of my nephew has come to me with a request to give protection to his son. When an enemy fails in battle or is disabled for some accidental reason, no truly brave warrior strike him. This is the *dharma* of a Kṣatriya. But what has happened to me now? My own sister is desperate, and requests me to protect her grandchild. Could there be a more pathetic situation than this?

If we go on analysing the various thoughts that were crowding in Arjuna's mind at that moment, surely there would be no limit to it. The language of a person whose heart is afflicted with so many thoughts and feelings becomes feeble and ineffective. Aware of the limits of language, the great poet only hints at the agitation in Arjuna's heart:

> *Evaṃ bruvatyāṃ karunam duhśalāyām dhaṇaṁjayaḥ/ Samṣmṛtya deviṃ gāndhārīm dhṛtarāṣṭraṁ ca pārthivam // uvāca duḥkhaśokartaḥ kṣatraḍharmaṁ vigarhayan/ Uhik taṁ duryodhanaṁ kṣudraṁ rājyalubdhaṁ ca mārninam// Yatkṛte bāndhaṿāḥ serve mayā nītā yamakṣayam/*

The great poet, who does not minimize his words on many other occasions, does not dare to say more here, but satisfies himself with two or three words: ***bahu***, ***sntvya***, and ***pariṣvajya***.

Arjuna is now drowned in the deep ocean of sorrow. Who can give him a helping hand and bring him to the shore? Could the words of consolation and courage which were addressed to him at the beginning of the fighting, when he was in a dejected mood, be helpful to him now? When calamities cloud the human spirit, no consoling or wise words make any impact. Kālidāsa knew this well. He says that when Aja fell into deep sorrow on the sudden death of his dear wife Indumatī, Vasiṣṭha sent his disciple to comfort him. The disciple delivered the message and went back, as if the message itself returned failing to enter the heart which was so filled with sorrow. *Tad albdhapadam hṛdi śokaghane pratiyātam ivāntikam asya guroḥ* (*Raghuvaṁśa*, 8).

After the *Mahābhārata* war only unpleasant circumstances surrounded the Pāṇḍavas. This started at Duryodhana's death when the gods praised him. Afterwards Yudhiṣṭhira realized that Karṇa was his own eldest brother for killing whom the Pāṇḍavas had had to resort to many unfair means. Then Yudhiṣṭhira had to fight his battle alone, a battle with his destiny and where bows, arrows or companions were of no avail. Then, of course, he performed the Aśvamedha only to be shown by a mongoose that it was not of a very high order as far as the results were concerned. It was not even equal in merit to one feeding of a Brāhmaṇa by a poor Brāhmaṇa family whose members had to starve after duly entertaining a poor guest. Imagine to what shame and anguish this must have put Yudhiṣṭhiras (*Āśvamedhika*, 92 and 93).

Now, Arjuna must have been as distressed as Yudhiṣṭhira at that point. By this time he had realized the unpleasant results of his proud Gāṇḍīva, the divine arrows and other divine weapons; he also realized that they did not serve any purpose at all. After the Vṛṣṇis, Andhakas and Yādavas destroyed themselves by foolishly fighting with each other and wiping out their race from the earth, and after Kṛṣṇa and Balarāma passed away the remaining women, children and elderly people were to be taken to Indraprastha by Arjuna before the sea swallowed Dvārakā. On the way, many hunters of Pāñcāladeśa obstructed their journey by carrying away the women under the care of Arjuna. Arjuna wanted to fight the hunters but alas! He found his arrows ineffective and he could not put even use his divine weapons (Mausala, 7). But even then he could not part with his weapons. He carried them along with him even when they started the Mahāprasthna. On the way, however, Agni appeared before him, and asked him to part with them. They were borrowed by Agni from Varuṇa on behalf of Arjuna for the Khāṇḍavadāha. Varuṇa was demanding them back. At last Arjuna threw them into the water. The poet reflects here on how difficult it is to loosen ones grip over the things which have been a cause of pride and prestige and to which one is deeply attached.

Though fortitude is the main sentiment pervading the great epic *Mahābhārata*, the subtle irony of the poet is evident throughout and perhaps all great poets share this attitude. They reflect on the vanity of the human race. In the *Mahābhārata*, Vyāsa smiles especially when he sees the vanity of Arjuna and Yudhiṣṭhira, although they were firm as far as *dharma* was concerned, and often acted righteously.

AN UNRESOLVED DILEMMA IN DYŪTA-PARVAN: A QUESTION RAISED BY DRAUPADĪ

S.M. KULKARNI

IN THE Dyūtaparvan under Sabhāparvan of the *Mahābhārata*, Draupadī, the Mahārāṇī of Pāṇḍavas raised an important question in the Assembly of Kauravas where she was brought by Duḥśāsana after she had been staked by Yudhiṣṭhira and been lost to Śakuni. It was a dilemma to all those who were present. Very few members attempted an answer to her question. Most of them preferred silence. Perhaps they were afraid of Duryodhana and his clique. There was no final answer to her question, and the dilemma remained unresolved. Even so, the question is important from the religious, moral, and social points of view. It involves a point of law also. Therefore, it will be worthwhile to discuss it, analyse it, and to find a solution, if possible. An attempt in that direction is made here. In doing so, the discussion which took place in the Kaurvasabhā will be helpful. Let us go through it.

When the *dyūta* or the play of dice began, Yudhiṣṭhira lost game after game and with it all the wealth in his possession which he betted. He then put on stake his brothers—Nakula, Sahadeva, Arjuna and Bhīmsena—one after another in that order, and lost all of them. Then Śakuni said to Yudhiṣṭhira:

बहु वित्तं पराजैषी-भ्रातृश्च सहयद्विपान्
आचक्ष्व वित्तं कौन्तेय यदि ते स्त्यपराजितम् ।।

O Son of Kunti ! You have lost almost all wealth including horses, elephants and also your brothers; now think and tell whether anything is left which is not lost yet.

To this Yudhiṣṭhira, putting himself at stake, answered.

'I am the eldest and beloved brother; I bet myself. If I lose I will do all that a slave does:'[1] There, like all previous games, Śakuni won this one also saying 'जितमित्येव' (I have won). It is clear that Śakuni had won Yudhiṣṭhira making him a slave. Then Śakuni said to Yudhiṣṭhira. 'O King! That you lost yourself is no good; because losing onself is a sin when some wealth is left there.'[2] Here it must be noted that Śakuni accepted that Yudhiṣṭhira had lost himself. His only contention was that it was bad. He even announced to all the kings present there that all the Pāṇḍavas had been lost.[3] Then again he said to Yudhiṣṭhira:

अस्ति ते वै प्रिया राजन् ग्लह एकोऽपराजितः
पणस्व कृष्णां पांचालीं तयाऽऽत्मानं पुनर्जय ।।

O King! There is still one thing left which is not lost yet; stake Pāñcālī Kṛṣṇā and get yourself conquered back thereby.

Here again Śakuni clearly stated that Yudhiṣṭhira had been conquered. At once Yudhiṣṭhira staked Draupadī. On hearing this there was the cry of 'shame'; 'shame' from all corners; kings felt sorry: Bhīṣma, Droṇa and Kripa perspired; Vidura, holding his head in his hands, almost became unconscious. It is noteworthy. though astonishing, that no one prevented Yudhiṣṭhira from betting Draupadī like that. Śakuni won this game also.

Winning this game meant winning Draupadī which, in turn, meant her becoming a *dāsī* (slave). This was the contention of Duryodhana and of all his fellows and followers. Immediately Duryodhana ordered Vidura to go and bring Draupadī to the *sabhā*. Vidura, of course, refused to do so. He announced that, according to him, Draupadī was not conquered at all. He said:

न हि दासीत्वमापन्ना कृष्णा भवितुमर्हति
अनीशेन हि राज्ञैषा पणे न्यस्तेति मे मतिः ।।

Draupadī cannot become *dāsī*, because Yudhiṣṭhira had no authority to bet her having first lost himself to Śakuni.

After this Duryodhana sent servant to Draupadī calling her to come to the court (*sabhā*). After hearing from him what had happened in the Kaurvasabhā, Draupadī asked him to go back and enquire from Yudhiṣṭhira whether he first lost himself or her.[4] By this Draupadī wanted to know whether she was really conquered or not. When ultimately she was dragged to the court (*sabhā*) by Duḥśāsana, her first question was whether the honourable members thought that according to law, she was conquered or not.[5] No one came forward to answer. Then Bhīṣma said: '*Dharma* being subtle I cannot quite properly analyse your question; no one who is not master can stake another's wealth; but wife is always under supremacy of her husband'.[6] Thus Bhīṣma indicated that, on the one hand, Yudhiṣṭhira by losing himself first had lost his authority over Draupadī and thus could not bet her; on the other hand, he believed that a husband's authority over his wife was never lost. So it was difficult to decide Draupadī's case. Bhīṣma further said that Yudhiṣṭhira, who never gave up *dharma* even though he may have to abandon the whole world, had admitted that he had been conquered. Therefore, he was unable to decide the point. This clearly shows that Bhīṣma knew, accepted, and gave importance to the fact that Yudhiṣṭhira had lost himself first, and then had put Draupadī on stake. A husband's authority over his wife not being clear, he had stated that he was unable to answer Draupadī's question. Bhīṣma further said: 'Śakuni is an expert in the game of dice. He induced Yudhiṣṭhira to put you at stake. But Yudhiṣṭhira does not think it as an act of deceit. Hence I cannot answer your question.'[8] A notable point arises from this that, if anyone fraudulently induces the other to act in a particular way, then that transaction becomes invalid. But, in that case, the complaint must come from the person concerned. In this case, Yudhiṣṭhira has no grudge. Therefore, nothing can be said and done. Draupadī probably got this point and stressed the same when she said:

> Experts in game, but mean, wicked, fraudulent and cunning gamblers began the play by inviting Yudhiṣṭhira, who had little practice of the game, to the court (*sabhā*) and induced him to play. Why was this? Those, whose intention is not pure and good, who are always busy in cheating others, first conquered Yudhiṣṭhira in the game and then compelled him to bet me.[9]

By this Draupadī wanted to indicate that the transaction being fraudulent and deceitful was not valid. Then, again, turning to the assembly she begged of them to answer her question clearly and properly. No one said anything. At last Vikarṇa, the younger brother of Duryodhana, got up and said that he felt it a bounden duty of a *sabhāsad* (member) to speak out his opinion. He emphatically stated:

> This son of Pāṇḍu, Yudhiṣṭhira, is addicted to the vice of gambling. He has bet Draupadī at the instance of cunning gamblers. Satī Draupadī is equally the wife of all Pāṇḍavas and not of Yudhiṣṭhira alone. Above all Yudhiṣṭhira lost himself first, and then put Draupadī on bet. Moreover, Śakuni, who was bent on winning each and every game, put forth the idea of betting Draupadī. Considering all these points I do not think Draupadī has been conquered.[10]

Four points emerge from this. They are:

(1) This transaction took place at the instance of others, while Yudhiṣṭhira was engrossed totally in the vice of gambling. Therefore, it was not valid.
(2) Draupadī being the wife of all the five Pāṇḍavas, Yudhiṣṭhira alone had no right to put her on stake. Hence the act without proper authority could not be accepted.
(3) Yudhiṣṭhira had himself lost first; therefore, he had no authority to stake Draupadī.
(4) Initial idea and suggestion was that of Śakuni and not of Yudhiṣṭhira. Hence this was a fraudulent act and stood nullified.

After Vikarṇa's speech there was no more valid point put forth by anybody. Duryodhana by way of giving concession to Draupadī, said to her that, if all the four Pāṇḍavas said clearly that Yudhiṣṭhira had no authority to put Draupadī on bet, then she would be freed. Bhīmasena spoke but did not say like that, and the other three kept silent. Yudhiṣṭhira also did not say anything, though Duryodhana (and again Bhīṣma) wanted him to say something. When Duryodhana repeated the same thing, Arjuna said that Yudhiṣṭhira had full authority to put us on stake before he lost himself. But when he himself was conquered, whose master did he remain? Let all Kauravas ponder over this.

This shows that, according to Arjuna, Dharamrāja had no authority over Draupadī to bet her after he had lost himself.

At this juncture, there were some bad omens in the *Yajñaśālā* of Dhṛtaraṣṭra. Apprehending some calamity, Vidura and Gāndharī went to Dhṛtarāṣṭra and apprised him of the situation. Taking serious not of it, Dhṛtarāṣṭra immediately stopped all proceedings, chided Duryodhana, and with due sympathy and respect granted boons one after another to his daughter-in-law, Mahārānī Draupadī. By one she asked release of Yudhiṣṭhira from the bondage, and by the second that of the other four Pāṇḍavas. Dhṛtarāṣṭra then ordered return of all wealth and the kingdom to Yudhiṣṭhira. Yudhiṣṭhira then returned to Indraprastha with full honour and authority. Here the first *dyūta* ended.

Let us now proceed to discuss in brief the main problem.

First of all, Vidura put forth his point clearly, viz. Yudhiṣṭhira having lost himself first had no authority to bet Draupadī. Bhīṣma also considered this as a valid point, though he had some doubt about the loss of paramountcy of husband over wife after the husband had been enslaved. Vikarṇa had supported this view. Arjuna also had thought this to be a valid point. All other members had kept silent due to the fear of Duryodhana. Therefore, the question of Draupadī had remained unanswered, officially.

Vikarṇa had put forth some more valid points. First of them concerns the validity of the act of an addict. Accordingly, the act of betting Draupadī by Yudhiṣṭhira is not valid, because, according to Vikarṇa, he was engrossed in gambling at that time. But, as Yudhiṣṭhira could not be called an addict in that sense, this point does not hold.

Draupadī was equally wedded to all the five Pāṇḍavas. Therefore, Yudhiṣṭhira alone had no authority to bet Draupadī. This is the second point of Vikarṇa and is valid one. But, as Pāṇḍavas themselves did not object on this count and accepted the authority of Yudhiṣṭhira, it could not be pressed.

Thirdly, a fraudulent and deceitful transaction cannot stand. Legally, this is a valid point. But here again the person concerned must say so and complain about it which, in this case, Yudhiṣṭhira did not.

Lastly, the question of the authority of the husband over his wife; is it limitless or ceases to be operative in certain circumstançes? This is a point to be considered. So far as this particular case is concerned, only Bhīṣma had expressed some doubt about it. Others did not expressly raise this point. But it can be inferred that they considered that Yuddhiṣṭhira had ceased to hold that authority over Draupadī after he had himself lost in the game.

It is important and interesting to note the opinion of Draupadī herself in this regard. She was asking whether she had been conquered or not conquered. To that end she wanted to know whether Yudhiṣṭhira first betted himself and lost or whether he betted her first. Although she came to know about this when she came to the court (*sabhā*), she wanted the verdict of the assembly and this she did not get. Ultimately, when Dhṛtarāṣṭra bestowed upon her boons, she wanted all the Pāṇḍavas to be freed. She never begged for her own freedom as she did not consider herself to have been conquered and enslaved. This clearly indicates that Yudhiṣṭhira had lost his authority over her as husband after he had lost himself to Śakuni.

Even so three points need consideration: (*i*) the nature of the authority of husband over wife; (*ii*) the validity of any act or transaction of an addict (though this does not/apply in this case); and (*iii*) the validity of any act fraudulently and deceitfully performed by cunning persons.

NOTES

1. अहं विशिष्टः सर्वेषां भ्रातृणां दयितस्तथा
   कुर्यामहं जितः कर्म स्वयमात्मन्युपप्लुते ॥—2-65-28
2. एतत् पापिष्ठमकरोर्यदात्मानमहारयः ॥
   शिष्टे सति धने राजन् पाप आत्मपराजयः ॥—2-65-30
3. एवं उक्त्वा मताक्षस्तान् ग्लहे सर्वानवस्थितान्
   पराजयं लोकवीरानुक्त्वा राज्ञां पृथक् पृथक् ॥—2-65-31
4. गच्छ त्वं कियवुं गत्वा सभायां पृच्छ सूतज
   किं नु पूर्वं पराजैषीरात्मानमथवा नु माम् ॥—2-67-7
5. जितां वाप्यजितां वा मां मन्यध्वे सर्वं भूमिपाः ॥—2-67-41
6. न धर्मसौक्ष्म्यात् सुभगे विवेक्तुं
   शक्नोमि ते प्रश्नमिमं यथावत्

अस्वाम्यशक्तः पणितुं परस्वं
स्त्रियाश्च भर्तुर्वशतां समीक्ष्य ॥—2-67-47

7. त्यजेत सर्वां पृथ्वीं समृद्धां
युधिष्ठिरो धर्ममथो न जह्यात्
उक्तं जितोऽस्मीति च पाण्डवेन
तस्मान्न शक्नोमि विवेक्तुमेतत् ॥—2-67-48

8. द्यूतेऽद्वितीयः शकुनिः नरेषु
कुन्तीसुतस्तेन निसृष्टकामः
न मन्यते तां निकृतिं युधिष्ठिर-
स्तस्मान्न ते प्रश्नमिमं ब्रवीमि ॥—2-67-49

9. आहूय राजा कुशलैरनार्यै-
र्दुष्टात्मभिर्नैकृतिकैः सभायाम्
द्यूतप्रियैर्नातिकृत प्रयत्नः
कस्मादयं नाम निसृष्टकामः ॥
अशुद्धभावैर्निकृतिप्रवृत्तै-
रबुध्यमानः कुरुपाण्डवाग्र्यः
सम्भूयसर्वैश्च जितोऽपि यस्मात्
पश्चादयं कैतवमभ्युपेतः ॥—2-67-50-51

10. तदयं पाण्डुपुत्रेण व्यसने वर्तता भृशम्
समाहूतेन कितवैरास्थितो द्रौपदीपणः ॥
साधारणी च सर्वेषां पाण्डवानामनिन्दिता
जितेन पूर्वानेन पाण्डवेन कृतः पणः ॥
इयं च कीर्तिता कृष्णा सौबलेन पणार्थिना
एतत् सर्वं विचार्याहं मन्ये न विजितामिमाम् ॥—2-68-22,23,24

11. ईशो राजा पूर्वमासीद् ग्लहे नः
कुन्तीसुतो धर्मराजो महात्मा
ईशस्त्वयं कस्य पराजितात्मा
तज्जानीध्वं कुरवः सर्व एव ॥—2-71-21

CONTRIBUTORS

M.M. AGRAWAL, Fellow, Indian Institute of Advanced Study, Shimla.

AMIYA DEV, Professor of Comparative Literature, Jadavpur University, Calcutta.

S.P. DUBEY, Reader in Philosophy, Rani Durgavati University, Jabalpur.

A.N. JANI, formerly Professor of Sanskrit, Prakrit and Pali, M.S. University, Baroda.

S.G. KANTAWALA, Professor of Sanskrit, Prakrit and Pali, M.S. University, Baroda.

S. PAUL KASHAP, Fellow, Indian Institute of Advanced Study, Shimla.

S.M. KULKARNI, formerly Professor of Marathi, S.B. City College, Nagpur.

BIMAL KRISHNA MATILAL, Spalding Professor of Eastern Religions and Ethics, All Souls College, Oxford.

K. KUNJUNNI RAJA, formerly Professor of Sanskrit, University of Madras, Madras.

T.S. RUKMANI, Principal, Miranda House, University of Delhi, Delhi.

PETER DELLA SANTINA, Fellow, Indian Institute of Advanced Study, Shimla.

E.R. SREEKRISHNA SARMA, Honorary Professor, Adyar Library and Research Centre, Adyar, Madras.

Y. KRISHAN, Fellow, Indian Council of Historical Research, New Delhi.